COLORADO

TRAVEL GUIDE 2024

Explore History, Culture, Hidden Gems, Cuisine and Local Secrets in the Centennial State – Packed with Detailed Maps & Travel Resources

BY

MICHAEL VIANNEY

Copyright © 2024 Michael Vianney. All rights reserved. The entirety of this material, encompassing text, visuals, and other multimedia elements, is the intellectual property of Michael Vianney and is safeguarded by copyright legislation and global agreements. No segment of this content may be replicated, shared, or transmitted in any form or via any medium without explicit written authorization from Michael Vianney. Unauthorized utilization, replication, or dispersal of this content may result in legal repercussions, encompassing civil and criminal penalties. For queries regarding permissions or additional information, kindly contact the author via the provided contact details in the publication or on the author's official page.

TABLE OF CONTENTS

Copyright.. 1
My Experience in Colorado..5
Why is Colorado a Must Visit?.......................................8
Key Features and Benefits of this Guide.....................11

Chapter 1. Introduction to Colorado........................... 16
1.1 Geography, Climate and Best Time to Visit.......... 16
1.2 History and Heritage... 19
1.3 Getting to Colorado...21
1.4 Local Etiquette and Customs................................24

Chapter 2. Accommodation Options...........................27
2.1 Hotels and Resorts... 27
2.2 Vacation Rentals...31
2.3 Bed and Breakfasts..34
2.4 Campgrounds and RV Parks................................ 39
2.5 Unique Accommodation Experiences...................42

Chapter 3. Transportation in Colorado...................... 47
3.1 Public Transportation..47
3.2 Rental Cars and Car Sharing................................49
3.3 Cycling and Bike Rentals......................................52
3.4 Taxi and Ride-Sharing Services...........................55
3.5 Driving Tips and Road Conditions........................ 58

Chapter 4. Top Attractions/Hidden Gems..................62
4.1 Must-Visit Landmarks... 62
4.2 Off-The-Beaten-Path Destinations.......................65

4.3 Scenic Drives and Byways..68
4.4 Local Festivals and Events.. 72
4.5 Unique Experiences and Activities......................................75

Chapter 5 Practical Information and Travel Resources.......... 79
5.1 Maps and Navigation... 79
5.2 Essential Packing List...81
5.3 Visa Requirements and Entry Procedures...........................84
5.4 Safety Tips and Emergency Contacts.................................86
5.5 Currency, Banking, Budgeting and Money Matters................88
5.6 Language, Communication and Useful Phrases....................91
5.7 Useful Websites, Mobile Apps and Online Resources............93
5.8 Visitor Centers and Tourist Assistance............................... 95

Chapter 6. Culinary Delights..99
6.1 Restaurants and Cafes... 99
6.2 Bars and Pubs... 102
6.3 Local Food Markets and Festivals.................................... 105
6.4 Culinary Tours and Classes... 109
6.5 Dietary Restrictions and Specialties..................................112

Chapter 7. Culture and Heritage.. 116
7.1 Museums and Galleries.. 116
7.2 Performing Arts and Theater..121
7.3 Indigenous Culture and Traditions................................... 125
7.4 Historic Sites and Monuments... 128
7.5 Artisan Communities and Workshops............................... 131

Chapter 8. Outdoor Activities and Adventures...................... 135
8.1 Hiking and Trekking... 135

8.2 Skiing and Snowboarding..138
8.3 Whitewater Rafting and Kayaking...144
8.4 Rock Climbing and Mountaineering.......................................147
8.5 Wildlife Watching and Nature Tours.....................................149

Chapter 9. Shopping in Colorado..151
9.1 Souvenirs and Gifts..151
9.2 Local Art and Craft Markets..153
9.3 Fashion and Apparel Boutiques..156
9.4 Antique Shops and Vintage Finds..159
9.5 Specialty Stores and Unique Finds......................................161

Chapter 10. Day Trips and Excursions.....................................164
10.1 Nearby Towns and Villages...164
10.2 National Parks and Recreation Areas...................................167
10.3 Scenic Drives and Road Trips..170
10.4 Adventure Tours and Excursions..173
10.5 Family-Friendly Day Outings...176

Chapter 11. Entertainment and Nightlife..................................179
11.1 Live Music Venues and Concerts..179
11.2 Performing Arts and Theatrical Performances...........................181
11.3 Nightclubs and Dance Floors...184
11.4 Comedy Clubs and Improv Shows...187
11.5 Late-Night Eateries and Hangouts......................................190
Closing Thoughts and Insider Tips..193

MY EXPERIENCE IN COLORADO

As a seasoned traveler and devoted author of travel guides, I've always believed in the power of firsthand experiences. My journey through Colorado was no exception, and it left an indelible mark on my soul. Let me take you on a vivid expedition through the breathtaking landscapes, vibrant cultures, and thrilling adventures that await in the heart of the Rockies.

My adventure began in the charming town of Boulder, nestled at the foothills of the Rocky Mountains. The crisp mountain air filled my lungs as I wandered through the bustling streets lined with quaint boutiques, cozy cafes, and vibrant street art. Every corner seemed to whisper tales of adventure and discovery, beckoning me to explore further. Next, I ventured into the majestic Rocky Mountain National Park, where towering peaks kissed the sky and alpine meadows stretched as far as the eye could see. As I hiked along winding trails, the beauty of the wilderness enveloped me, leaving me awestruck at every turn. The sound of rushing waterfalls and the scent of pine trees filled my senses, reminding me of the raw power and boundless beauty of nature.

One of the highlights of my journey was experiencing the vibrant culture of Denver, the Mile High City. From the bustling streets of LoDo to the trendy neighborhoods of RiNo, Denver pulsates with energy and creativity. I immersed myself in the local art scene, exploring galleries and street murals that showcased the city's eclectic spirit. And no visit to Denver would be complete without sampling its renowned craft beer scene – each sip a testament to the passion and innovation of Colorado's brewers. But it was in the small mountain towns scattered throughout the state that I truly discovered the heart and soul of Colorado. From the historic mining town of Telluride to the artistic enclave of Crested Butte, each town had its own unique charm and character. I found myself drawn to the warmth and hospitality of the locals, who welcomed me with open arms and shared their stories of life in the Rockies.

Of course, no visit to Colorado would be complete without indulging in some adrenaline-pumping adventures. Whether it was whitewater rafting down the rapids of the Arkansas River or soaring high above the mountains on a thrilling zip line, I found myself constantly pushing the boundaries of my comfort zone and embracing the thrill of the unknown. But amidst the excitement and adventure, there were also moments of quiet reflection and serenity. Watching the sunset paint the sky in shades of orange and pink from the summit of a mountain peak, or gazing up at a blanket of stars shimmering in the night sky – these were the moments that reminded me of the awe-inspiring beauty and majesty of the natural world.

As I reflect on my journey through Colorado, I am filled with a sense of gratitude and wonder. It is a place that has captured my heart and ignited my spirit of adventure. From the rugged beauty of the mountains to the vibrant culture of its cities and towns,

Colorado is a destination like no other – a place where every moment is an opportunity for discovery and exploration. So, to all those who seek adventure and yearn to explore the unknown, I urge you to pack your bags and embark on your own journey through the heart of the Rockies. Let Colorado captivate your imagination, inspire your soul, and leave you forever changed. The adventure of a lifetime awaits – are you ready to answer the call?

WHY IS COLORADO A MUST VISIT?

Colorado, often hailed as the crown jewel of the Rocky Mountains, beckons travelers with its mesmerizing landscapes and unparalleled natural beauty. From rugged mountain peaks to cascading waterfalls, expansive plains to crystal-clear lakes, Colorado is a haven for outdoor enthusiasts and nature lovers alike. The sheer diversity of its terrain promises a wealth of experiences waiting to be discovered.

Outdoor Adventures

For those who crave adventure, Colorado offers an endless array of thrilling outdoor activities. Whether it's skiing down powdery slopes in world-class resorts like Aspen and Vail, hiking through pristine wilderness in Rocky Mountain National Park, or embarking on a whitewater rafting expedition down the roaring rapids of the Arkansas River, there's something for every adrenaline junkie in Colorado. And for those seeking a more leisurely pace, the state's numerous hiking trails, scenic drives, and wildlife viewing opportunities provide ample opportunities to reconnect with nature.

A Cultural Tapestry

Beyond its natural wonders, Colorado is also a melting pot of cultures and traditions. From the vibrant arts scene in cities like Denver and Boulder to the rich Native American heritage found in places like Mesa Verde National Park, Colorado offers a glimpse into the diverse tapestry of human experience. Visitors can explore historic mining towns, attend festivals celebrating everything from craft beer to cowboy culture, and immerse themselves in the creative energy of local artists and musicians.

Seasonal Splendor

One of the most magical aspects of Colorado is its distinct seasons, each offering its own unique charm and beauty. In the winter, the state transforms into a winter wonderland, with snow-capped mountains and frost-covered forests providing the perfect backdrop for skiing, snowboarding, and cozying up by the fire. Spring brings a burst of color as wildflowers blanket the alpine meadows, while summer invites visitors to bask in the warm sunshine and explore the great outdoors. And in the fall, the mountains come alive with a kaleidoscope of reds, yellows, and oranges as the aspen trees change color, creating a breathtaking spectacle that must be seen to be believed.

Legendary Hospitality

But perhaps what sets Colorado apart is its legendary hospitality and welcoming spirit. Whether you're sharing stories with locals at a mountain tavern, enjoying a home-cooked meal at a bed and breakfast, or simply striking up a conversation with a fellow hiker on the trail, you'll find that the people of Colorado are as warm and inviting as the landscapes they call home. It's this sense of community and camaraderie that leaves a lasting impression on visitors and keeps them coming back year after year.

Colorado is more than just a destination – it's an experience that touches the soul and leaves a lasting imprint on the heart. With its boundless beauty, endless adventures, rich culture, and warm hospitality, Colorado is a must-visit destination for anyone seeking to be inspired, rejuvenated, and truly alive. So pack your bags, hit the road, and let Colorado work its magic on you. You won't be disappointed.

KEY FEATURES AND BENEFITS OF THIS GUIDE

Welcome to the **"Colorado Travel Guide 2024,"** your ultimate companion to unlocking the essence of this captivating state. As an author with a wealth of experience in crafting travel guides, I've poured my heart and soul into curating a comprehensive resource that goes beyond the surface to reveal the true essence of Colorado. Whether you're a first-time traveler or a seasoned explorer, this guide is your ticket to discovering the hidden gems, iconic landmarks, and unforgettable experiences that await in the Centennial State.

Maps and Navigation:

Embarking on your Colorado adventure is made effortless with detailed maps and navigation tips included in this guide. From the bustling streets of Denver to the remote trails of Rocky Mountain National Park, you'll have access to comprehensive maps that ensure you never lose your way. Insider tips on navigating mountain passes, scenic byways, and public transportation options will help you make the most of your journey across this diverse landscape.

Accommodation Options:

Finding the perfect place to rest your head is essential for a memorable Colorado experience, and this guide has you covered. From luxury resorts nestled in the heart of ski towns to cozy cabins tucked away in secluded mountain valleys, you'll find a range of accommodation options to suit every taste and budget. Insider recommendations, reviews, and booking tips ensure that you find the perfect home base for your Colorado adventure.

Transportation:

Navigating Colorado's vast terrain is made seamless with comprehensive transportation information provided in this guide. Whether you're flying into Denver International Airport, renting a car to explore the Rocky Mountains, or hopping on a scenic train ride through the Colorado countryside, you'll find all the information you need to plan your journey with confidence. Insider tips on road conditions, driving routes, and alternative transportation options ensure smooth sailing throughout your travels.

Must-See Sights and Hidden Gems

Colorado is home to a wealth of top attractions and hidden gems just waiting to be discovered, and this guide highlights them all. From iconic landmarks like Garden of the Gods and Mesa Verde National Park to off-the-beaten-path treasures like Great Sand Dunes National Park and Black Canyon of the Gunnison National Park, you'll uncover the true essence of Colorado's natural beauty and cultural heritage. Insider tips on avoiding crowds, best times to visit, and unique experiences ensure that you make the most of your time in the Centennial State.

Practical Information and Travel Resources:

Preparing for your Colorado adventure is made simple with practical information and travel resources provided in this guide. From packing essentials for outdoor adventures to safety tips for navigating mountain terrain, you'll find everything you need to know to travel with confidence. Insider recommendations for local services, emergency contacts, and travel insurance ensure that you have peace of mind throughout your journey.

Tasting the Flavors of Colorado

No visit to Colorado is complete without indulging in its culinary delights, and this guide introduces you to the state's vibrant food scene. From farm-to-table restaurants serving up fresh, local cuisine to craft breweries pouring innovative beers, you'll discover a world of flavors that reflect Colorado's diverse landscape and cultural heritage. Insider recommendations for must-try dishes, hidden gems, and food festivals ensure that you savor every moment of your culinary adventure.

Culture and Heritage:

Delve into Colorado's rich history and cultural heritage with insights provided in this guide. From Native American traditions to the legacy of the mining era, you'll gain a deeper understanding of the people and places that have shaped the Centennial State. Insider tips on cultural attractions, heritage sites, and immersive experiences ensure that you connect with Colorado's past in meaningful ways.

Outdoor Activities and Adventures:

Embark on unforgettable outdoor adventures with the guidance of this comprehensive guide. Whether you're skiing down pristine slopes, hiking through alpine meadows, or rafting down rushing rivers, you'll find endless opportunities to embrace the spirit of adventure in Colorado. Insider recommendations for outdoor activities, gear rentals, and guided tours ensure that you make the most of your time in the great outdoors.

Shopping:

Indulge in retail therapy with insider tips on shopping destinations provided in this guide. From quaint boutiques in mountain towns to bustling markets in urban centers, you'll find a treasure trove of unique gifts and souvenirs to commemorate your Colorado adventure. Insider recommendations for artisanal crafts, local products, and hidden gems ensure that you bring home a piece of Colorado's charm.

Day Trips and Excursions:

Venture off the beaten path with day trip and excursion ideas offered in this guide. From scenic drives along winding mountain roads to explorations of nearby attractions and hidden gems, you'll discover a wealth of opportunities to expand your Colorado adventure. Insider recommendations for day trip itineraries, transportation options, and hidden gems ensure that you make the most of your time exploring the Centennial State.

Entertainment and Nightlife:

Experience Colorado's vibrant entertainment and nightlife scene with recommendations provided in this guide. From live music venues and theater productions to lively bars and clubs, you'll find endless opportunities to unwind and socialize after dark. Insider tips on local hotspots, upcoming events, and nightlife districts ensure that you make the most of your evenings in Colorado.

The **"Colorado Travel Guide 2024"** is your indispensable companion to unlocking the essence of the Centennial State. With detailed information on maps and navigation, accommodation options, transportation, top attractions, practical tips, culinary delights, cultural experiences, outdoor adventures, shopping destinations, day trips, and nightlife, this guide ensures that you have everything you need to embark on an unforgettable journey through Colorado.

CHAPTER 1

INTRODUCTION TO COLORADO

1.1 Geography, Climate and Best Time to Visit

Welcome to Colorado, a state in Denver, United States, renowned for its diverse geography, dynamic climate, and stunning natural beauty. As you prepare to embark on your journey to the Centennial State, allow me to guide you through the rich tapestry of geography, climate, and seasonal charms that await you.

Geography:

Colorado's geography is characterized by its dramatic contrasts, with rugged mountain peaks, vast plains, and everything in between. The Rocky Mountains dominate the western half of the state, with towering summits, deep valleys, and alpine lakes creating a playground for outdoor enthusiasts. To the east, the landscape gradually flattens into the Great Plains, where rolling prairies and expansive farmland stretch as far as the eye can see. In between, you'll find a diverse array of ecosystems, including forests, deserts, canyons, and wetlands, each offering its own unique beauty and opportunities for exploration.

Climate:
Colorado's climate is as varied and dynamic as its geography, with distinct regional differences influenced by elevation, geography, and prevailing weather patterns. Generally, the state experiences a semi-arid climate, with low humidity and abundant sunshine throughout the year. However, temperatures and weather conditions can vary dramatically depending on location and season. In the mountains, temperatures are cooler and more variable, with snowfall possible year-round at higher elevations. In the eastern plains, temperatures are warmer and more stable, with hot summers and cold winters. The state's diverse microclimates mean that weather conditions can change rapidly, so it's essential to be prepared for a wide range of conditions, especially if you plan to explore different regions during your visit.

Best Time to Visit:
Choosing the best time to visit Colorado depends on your interests and preferred activities, as each season offers its own unique attractions and experiences.

Spring (March-May): Spring is a magical time in Colorado, as the landscape comes alive with blooming wildflowers, rushing waterfalls, and vibrant greenery. It's an ideal time for hiking, wildlife viewing, and exploring the state's national parks and scenic drives. Be prepared for variable weather conditions, including potential snowfall at higher elevations.

Summer (June-August): Summer is peak season in Colorado, with warm temperatures, long days, and endless opportunities for outdoor adventure. From hiking and camping in the mountains to rafting and fishing in the rivers, there's no shortage of activities to enjoy. Popular destinations like Rocky Mountain National Park and the ski resorts of Aspen and Vail come alive with visitors, so be sure to book accommodations and activities in advance.

Fall (September-November): Fall is a spectacular time to visit Colorado, as the mountains are transformed into a kaleidoscope of autumn colors. The aspen trees turn vibrant shades of gold, orange, and red, creating a breathtaking backdrop for hiking, photography, and scenic drives. It's also harvest season, with farmers markets, apple orchards, and pumpkin patches offering a taste of local bounty.

Winter (December-February): Winter is synonymous with skiing and snowboarding in Colorado, as the state boasts some of the best ski resorts in the country. From world-class slopes in Aspen and Breckenridge to family-friendly resorts like Keystone and

Winter Park, there's a ski destination to suit every skill level and budget. Beyond the slopes, winter activities like snowshoeing, ice skating, and hot springs soaking offer plenty of opportunities for outdoor fun.

1.2 History and Heritage

Colorado is a city where the echoes of centuries past reverberate through the rugged landscapes and historic landmarks of the Centennial State. From ancient Native American cultures to the pioneering spirit of the Wild West, Colorado's past is a vibrant mosaic of stories, struggles, and triumphs that have shaped the identity of the Centennial State. As you explore the historic sites, museums, and cultural landmarks scattered across Colorado's landscape, you'll uncover the layers of history that have left an indelible mark on this land and its people.

Native American Heritage:

Long before European settlers arrived, Colorado was home to a rich tapestry of Native American cultures, each leaving their own imprint on the land. From the Ancestral Puebloans who built elaborate cliff dwellings at Mesa Verde to the Ute, Cheyenne, Arapaho, and other tribes who roamed the plains and mountains, Colorado's indigenous peoples lived in harmony with the land for thousands of years. Today, visitors can explore archaeological sites, museums, and cultural centers that preserve and celebrate the heritage of Colorado's Native American communities.

Exploration and Expansion:

The 19th century brought waves of exploration and settlement to Colorado, as pioneers and prospectors flocked to the region in search of gold, silver, and new opportunities. The discovery of gold in 1858 sparked the famous Colorado Gold Rush, drawing fortune seekers from around the world to towns like Denver, Central City, and Leadville. As settlers established homesteads, ranches, and mining camps across the state, Colorado's population boomed, bringing with it a wave of innovation, entrepreneurship, and cultural diversity.

The Wild West:

Colorado's history is steeped in the lore of the Wild West, where cowboys, outlaws, and frontiersmen roamed the untamed landscape. Towns like Durango, Telluride, and Gunnison were once bustling hubs of cowboy culture, where cattle drives, saloons, and shootouts were a way of life. Notorious outlaws like Butch Cassidy and the Sundance Kid left their mark on Colorado's history, while legendary figures like Buffalo Bill Cody and Kit Carson became synonymous with the spirit of the American West.

Mining and Industry:

The mining industry played a pivotal role in Colorado's history, shaping the state's economy, culture, and landscape. From the silver mines of Leadville to the coal mines of Trinidad, Colorado's mineral wealth fueled rapid growth and development in the late 19th and early 20th centuries. Towns sprung up overnight, railroads crisscrossed the state, and fortunes were made and lost in the blink of an eye. But with prosperity came challenges, as mining accidents, labor strikes, and environmental degradation underscored the high stakes of Colorado's industrial boom.

Conservation and Preservation:
Amidst the rapid development and exploitation of Colorado's natural resources, a conservation movement emerged to protect the state's pristine wilderness and natural beauty. Visionary leaders like Enos Mills and John Muir advocated for the creation of national parks and wilderness areas, leading to the establishment of iconic landmarks like Rocky Mountain National Park, Mesa Verde National Park, and the Maroon Bells-Snowmass Wilderness. Today, Colorado's conservation legacy continues, with efforts to preserve and protect the state's natural heritage for future generations.

1.3 Getting to Colorado

As you prepare to embark on your adventure to Colorado, it's essential to consider the best ways to reach this captivating destination. Whether you're traveling from across the country or around the globe, there are several convenient options for reaching the Centennial State.

By Air:
For many travelers, flying into one of Colorado's major airports is the most convenient and efficient way to reach the state. Denver

International Airport (DEN) serves as the primary gateway to Colorado, offering a wide range of domestic and international flights from major airlines such as United, American, Delta, and Southwest. Located just 25 miles northeast of downtown Denver, DEN provides easy access to the city and serves as a hub for connecting flights to destinations across the state. In addition to Denver, Colorado is also served by several regional airports, including Colorado Springs Airport (COS), Aspen-Pitkin County Airport (ASE), Eagle County Regional Airport (EGE), and Durango-La Plata County Airport (DRO). These airports offer convenient access to popular destinations such as Colorado Springs, Aspen, Vail, and Durango, allowing travelers to bypass the hustle and bustle of larger airports and arrive directly at their final destination. When booking flights to Colorado, it's advisable to compare prices and availability across multiple airlines and travel websites to ensure you find the best deals. Websites like Expedia, Kayak, and Google Flights allow you to search for flights, compare prices, and book tickets online, making it easy to plan your journey with ease.

By Train:

For travelers seeking a more scenic and leisurely journey, riding the rails to Colorado can be a memorable and enjoyable experience. Amtrak offers train service to several cities in Colorado, including Denver, Colorado Springs, and Grand Junction, with routes such as the California Zephyr and the Southwest Chief providing connections from cities across the country. The California Zephyr, in particular, is renowned for its breathtaking views as it winds its way through the Rocky Mountains, offering passengers a front-row seat to some of Colorado's most iconic scenery. From towering peaks to winding rivers, the journey aboard the California Zephyr is a testament to the beauty and majesty of the American West. When planning your train journey to Colorado, be sure to check Amtrak's website for schedules, fares, and ticket availability. It's also advisable to book tickets in advance, especially during peak travel times, to ensure you secure your preferred travel dates and accommodations.

By Road:

For those who prefer the freedom and flexibility of traveling by car, hitting the road to Colorado offers the opportunity to explore the state's scenic landscapes at your own pace. Colorado is easily accessible by major interstate highways, including I-25, I-70, and I-76, which connect the state to neighboring states such as Wyoming, Nebraska, and New Mexico. If you're traveling from nearby states such as Utah, Arizona, or Kansas, driving to Colorado can be a relatively straightforward journey, with scenic routes and picturesque vistas along the way. For longer distances, consider breaking up your drive with overnight stops in charming towns and cities along the route, allowing you to experience the local culture and hospitality of the American West. Before embarking on your road trip to Colorado, be sure to plan your route in advance and check road conditions, especially during winter months when snow and ice can affect travel. Additionally, consider renting a car from one of the major car rental companies such as Hertz, Avis, or Enterprise, which offer convenient pickup and drop-off locations at airports and cities across the state.

1.4 Local Etiquette and Customs

As you prepare to immerse yourself in the vibrant culture and welcoming atmosphere of Colorado, understanding local etiquette and customs is essential for ensuring a respectful and enjoyable experience. From mountain towns to bustling cities, Coloradoans take pride in their unique customs, traditions, and way of life. By embracing these customs, you'll not only show respect for the local culture but also enhance your connection to the people and places you encounter during your visit to the Centennial State.

Respect for Nature:

Coloradoans have a deep reverence for the natural beauty that surrounds them, and respecting the environment is a fundamental aspect of local etiquette. Whether you're hiking in the mountains, exploring a national park, or simply strolling through a city park, be sure to leave no trace by properly disposing of trash, staying on designated trails, and avoiding activities that could harm the local ecosystem. By practicing responsible outdoor etiquette, you'll help preserve Colorado's pristine landscapes for future generations to enjoy.

Embracing the Colorado Lifestyle

Coloradoans are known for their casual and laid-back attitude, and visitors are encouraged to embrace this relaxed vibe during their stay. Whether you're dining at a local restaurant, shopping in a boutique, or striking up a conversation with a stranger, feel free to let your guard down and enjoy the friendly, down-to-earth atmosphere that permeates Colorado's communities. A smile, a friendly greeting, and a genuine interest in others go a long way in fostering connections and building rapport with locals.

Outdoor Adventures Etiquette:

With its abundance of outdoor recreational opportunities, Colorado is a playground for outdoor enthusiasts of all kinds. Whether you're hiking, biking, skiing, or snowboarding, it's important to observe proper trail and slope etiquette to ensure a safe and enjoyable experience for everyone. Be courteous to other trail users, yield to uphill traffic, and obey posted signs and rules. Additionally, when skiing or snowboarding, be mindful of your speed and control, and respect the natural environment by avoiding off-trail areas and preserving fragile alpine ecosystems.

Tipping Culture:

In Colorado, tipping is customary in restaurants, bars, and other service industries as a way to show appreciation for good service. Standard tipping practices typically range from 15% to 20% of the total bill, depending on the level of service received. It's also common to tip hotel staff, tour guides, and other service providers for exceptional service. When in doubt, err on the side of generosity and tip accordingly, knowing that your gratuity is a direct expression of gratitude for the hard work and dedication of those who serve you.

Dress Code:
Colorado's diverse climate and outdoor-oriented lifestyle mean that dressing in layers is key to staying comfortable and prepared for changing weather conditions. Whether you're exploring the mountains, strolling through a city, or dining at a restaurant, it's wise to dress in casual, practical clothing that can easily transition from day to night.

CHAPTER 2
ACCOMMODATION OPTIONS

Click the link or Scan QR Code with a device to view a comprehensive map of various Accommodation Options in Colorado – https://shorturl.at/cgK12

2.1 Hotels and Resorts

Colorado, with its stunning mountain landscapes and vibrant culture, offers a plethora of luxurious accommodations for visitors seeking a memorable stay. From charming boutique hotels nestled in quaint mountain towns to lavish resorts boasting world-class amenities, there's something to suit every traveler's taste. Here's some exquisite hotels and resorts in Colorado that promise an unforgettable experience.

The Broadmoor

Nestled at the foot of the majestic Cheyenne Mountain in Colorado Springs, The Broadmoor stands as an icon of luxury and elegance. This historic resort, founded in 1918, offers timeless charm and impeccable service. With a variety of accommodation options, including spacious rooms, suites, and cottages, The Broadmoor caters to every guest's needs. Prices for lodging vary depending on the season and room type, with rates typically ranging from $300 to $800 per night. Guests at The Broadmoor can indulge in a wealth of amenities, including three championship golf courses, an award-winning spa, and an array of dining options ranging from casual to fine dining. Adventure seekers will appreciate the resort's proximity to outdoor activities such as hiking, horseback riding, and fly fishing. With its historic charm, stunning mountain views, and unparalleled service, The Broadmoor promises a truly luxurious retreat. Official website for booking and reservations: https://resv.broadmoor.com/

The Little Nell

Situated at the base of Aspen Mountain, The Little Nell epitomizes luxury in the heart of Aspen. This five-star, five-diamond hotel offers unparalleled access to world-class skiing, shopping, and dining. The Little Nell features beautifully appointed rooms and suites with elegant mountain-inspired décor, each offering breathtaking views of the surrounding peaks. Prices for lodging at The Little Nell typically range from $600 to $2000 per night, depending on the room category and season. Guests at The Little Nell can enjoy a host of amenities, including a renowned fine dining restaurant, a heated outdoor pool and hot tubs, and a full-service fitness center. The hotel also offers personalized services such as ski concierge and in-room dining to ensure a truly luxurious experience. Whether hitting the slopes in the winter or exploring the vibrant Aspen scene in the summer, The Little Nell provides the perfect base for a memorable mountain getaway. Official website for booking and reservations: https://www.thelittlenell.com/

Dunton Hot Springs

Tucked away in the rugged San Juan Mountains near Telluride, Dunton Hot Springs offers a secluded and luxurious retreat in a breathtaking natural setting. This exclusive resort, comprising beautifully restored 19th-century cabins and a charming main lodge, combines rustic elegance with modern comforts. Prices for lodging at Dunton Hot Springs vary depending on the accommodation type and season, with rates typically ranging from $1000 to $3000 per night. Guests at Dunton Hot Springs can unwind in natural hot springs, enjoy gourmet meals prepared with locally sourced ingredients, and explore the surrounding wilderness through activities such as hiking, horseback riding, and fly fishing. The resort also offers wellness retreats, yoga classes, and spa services for those seeking relaxation and rejuvenation. With its serene ambiance and unparalleled natural beauty, Dunton Hot Springs is a hidden gem for discerning travelers seeking a unique and immersive experience. Official website for booking and reservations: https://www.duntondestinations.com/hot-springs/

The Ritz-Carlton

Perched high above the scenic Beaver Creek Mountain, The Ritz-Carlton, Bachelor Gulch offers a luxurious mountain retreat in the heart of Colorado's Rocky Mountains. This elegant resort boasts spacious rooms and suites with stunning mountain views, as well as luxurious amenities and personalized service. Prices for lodging at The Ritz-Carlton, Bachelor Gulch typically range from $500 to $1500 per night, depending on the room type and season. Guests at The Ritz-Carlton, Bachelor Gulch can enjoy access to world-class skiing, hiking trails, and outdoor adventures right at their doorstep. The resort also features a spa, fitness center, and multiple dining options, including a signature restaurant serving seasonal mountain cuisine. Whether seeking adventure on the slopes or relaxation in a serene mountain setting, The Ritz-Carlton, Bachelor Gulch offers the perfect blend of luxury and natural beauty. Official website for booking and reservations: https://www.ritzcarlton.com/en/

The Stanley Hotel
Nestled in the picturesque town of Estes Park, The Stanley Hotel is a historic landmark renowned for its stunning architecture and breathtaking mountain views. This grand hotel, built in 1909, offers a unique blend of old-world charm and modern amenities. Prices for lodging at The Stanley Hotel vary depending on the room type and season, with rates typically ranging from $200 to $600 per night. Guests at The Stanley Hotel can explore the nearby Rocky Mountain National Park, enjoy live music and entertainment at the hotel's various venues, or simply relax on the expansive verandas overlooking the mountains. The hotel also offers guided ghost tours for those interested in its rich history and paranormal

legends. With its scenic location, historic ambiance, and range of activities, The Stanley Hotel offers a memorable retreat for guests seeking a quintessential Colorado experience. Official website for booking and reservations: https://www.stanleyhotel.com/

2.2 Vacation Rentals

Colorado's diverse landscapes and vibrant culture make it an ideal destination for travelers seeking a unique vacation experience. Whether you're looking for a cozy cabin retreat in the mountains or a chic urban loft in the heart of a bustling city, Colorado offers a plethora of vacation rental options to suit every taste and budget. Here's some exceptional vacation rentals in Colorado that promise a memorable and comfortable stay.

Mountain Majesty Cabin
Tucked away in the picturesque town of Breckenridge, Mountain Majesty Cabin offers a tranquil retreat amidst the stunning Rocky Mountains. This charming vacation rental features a cozy interior with wood-paneled walls, a stone fireplace, and panoramic views of the surrounding forest. Prices for lodging at Mountain Majesty Cabin vary depending on the season and duration of stay, with rates typically ranging from $200 to $500 per night. Guests at Mountain Majesty Cabin can enjoy a range of amenities, including a fully equipped kitchen, outdoor hot tub, and spacious deck ideal for soaking in the mountain scenery. The cabin's proximity to outdoor activities such as skiing, hiking, and mountain biking makes it an ideal base for adventure seekers. Whether you're

curling up by the fire with a good book or exploring the natural beauty of the Rockies, Mountain Majesty Cabin offers a cozy and memorable mountain retreat.

Denver Urban Loft

For travelers seeking a chic and contemporary urban getaway, the Denver Urban Loft offers a stylish retreat in the heart of Colorado's capital city. Located in the trendy LoDo (Lower Downtown) neighborhood, this spacious loft features modern design elements, high ceilings, and floor-to-ceiling windows offering sweeping views of the city skyline. Prices for lodging at the Denver Urban Loft vary depending on the season and length of stay, with rates typically ranging from $150 to $400 per night. Guests at the Denver Urban Loft can enjoy a range of amenities, including a fully equipped kitchen, comfortable living area, and access to a rooftop deck with panoramic views of downtown Denver. The loft's prime location puts guests within walking distance of top attractions, including Coors Field, Union Station, and the vibrant restaurant and nightlife scene of LoDo. Whether you're exploring the city's cultural landmarks or simply soaking in the urban atmosphere, the Denver Urban Loft offers a stylish and convenient home base for your Colorado adventure.

Aspen Luxury Chalet

Nestled in the exclusive enclave of Aspen, the Aspen Luxury Chalet offers discerning travelers a lavish mountain retreat with unparalleled amenities and service. This opulent vacation rental features spacious living areas, designer furnishings, and panoramic views of the surrounding mountains. Prices for lodging at the Aspen Luxury Chalet vary depending on the season and duration of stay, with rates typically ranging from $1000 to $5000 per night. Guests at the Aspen Luxury Chalet can indulge in a range of amenities, including a private hot tub, gourmet kitchen, and home theater system. The chalet's prime location puts guests within easy reach of Aspen's world-class skiing, shopping, and dining opportunities. Whether you're hitting the slopes in the winter or exploring the scenic beauty of the Rockies in the summer, the Aspen Luxury Chalet offers a luxurious and unforgettable mountain getaway. Official website for booking and reservations: https://www.aspenluxuryvacationrentals.com/

Boulder Mountain Retreat
Escape to the tranquility of the Colorado foothills with a stay at the Boulder Mountain Retreat. Located just outside the vibrant city of Boulder, this charming vacation rental offers a peaceful retreat surrounded by nature. The retreat features cozy accommodations with rustic decor, a fully equipped kitchen, and a private deck overlooking the forest. Prices for lodging at the Boulder Mountain Retreat vary depending on the season and length of stay, with rates typically ranging from $150 to $400 per night. Guests at the Boulder Mountain Retreat can enjoy a range of outdoor activities, including hiking, mountain biking, and wildlife viewing. The retreat's serene setting provides the perfect opportunity to unwind and reconnect with nature, while still being within easy reach of

Boulder's cultural attractions and amenities. Whether you're seeking adventure in the great outdoors or simply seeking a peaceful escape from the hustle and bustle of city life, the Boulder Mountain Retreat offers the perfect retreat.

Telluride Ski Chalet

Experience the ultimate mountain getaway with a stay at the Telluride Ski Chalet. Nestled in the heart of Telluride's ski resort, this luxurious vacation rental offers ski-in/ski-out access and breathtaking views of the surrounding peaks. The chalet features upscale furnishings, a gourmet kitchen, and a cozy fireplace perfect for après-ski relaxation. Prices for lodging at the Telluride Ski Chalet vary depending on the season and duration of stay, with rates typically ranging from $500 to $1500 per night. Guests at the Telluride Ski Chalet can enjoy a range of amenities, including a private hot tub, media room, and ski concierge service. The chalet's prime location puts guests within easy reach of Telluride's world-class skiing, dining, and shopping opportunities. Whether you're hitting the slopes in the winter or exploring the mountain trails in the summer, the Telluride Ski Chalet offers a luxurious and convenient mountain retreat. Official website for booking and reservations: https://tellurideskiresort.com/

2.3 Bed and Breakfasts

Nestled amidst the majestic Rocky Mountains, Colorado offers a wealth of charming bed and breakfasts, each providing a unique blend of hospitality, comfort, and scenic beauty. These cozy retreats beckon travelers seeking a more intimate and personalized lodging experience, whether they're exploring the state's natural wonders or immersing themselves in its vibrant culture.

Highland Haven Creekside Inn

Located in the enchanting town of Evergreen, Highland Haven Creekside Inn offers a serene escape amidst towering pine trees and the soothing sounds of Bear Creek. This rustic yet elegant bed and breakfast features beautifully appointed rooms and cottages, each uniquely decorated with handcrafted furnishings and luxurious amenities. Prices for lodging at Highland Haven vary depending on the season and accommodation type, with rates typically ranging from $200 to $400 per night. Guests at Highland Haven can enjoy a range of amenities, including a gourmet breakfast served daily, complimentary wine and cheese receptions, and access to private hiking trails along Bear Creek. The inn's picturesque setting provides the perfect backdrop for outdoor activities such as hiking, fishing, and wildlife viewing. Whether you're seeking a romantic retreat or a peaceful getaway in nature, Highland Haven Creekside Inn offers a warm and welcoming atmosphere for guests to unwind and recharge. Website for booking and reservations: https://highlandhaven.com/

The Cliff House at Pikes Peak

Perched atop a bluff overlooking the historic town of Manitou Springs, The Cliff House at Pikes Peak offers luxurious accommodations in a stunning natural setting. This elegant bed and breakfast, originally built in 1873, has been meticulously restored to its former glory, blending Victorian charm with modern comforts. Prices for lodging at The Cliff House vary depending on the season and room category, with rates typically ranging from $250 to $600 per night. Guests at The Cliff House can indulge in a range of amenities, including a gourmet breakfast served in the hotel's award-winning dining room, afternoon tea in the cozy parlor, and access to a rooftop terrace with panoramic views of Pikes Peak. The bed and breakfast's prime location puts guests within easy reach of Manitou Springs' attractions, including historic landmarks, art galleries, and outdoor adventures. Whether you're exploring the nearby Garden of the Gods or simply relaxing on the veranda with a glass of wine, The Cliff House at Pikes Peak offers a luxurious retreat for discerning travelers. Official website for booking and reservations: https://www.thecliffhouse.com/

Castle Marne Bed & Breakfast

Step back in time to the elegant Victorian era with a stay at Castle Marne Bed & Breakfast in Denver's historic Capitol Hill neighborhood. This grand mansion, built in 1889, exudes old-world charm and sophistication, with beautifully restored rooms and suites featuring period furnishings and modern amenities. Prices for lodging at Castle Marne vary depending on the season and room category, with rates typically ranging from $200 to $500 per night. Guests at Castle Marne can enjoy a range of amenities, including a gourmet breakfast served in the opulent dining room, afternoon tea in the cozy parlor, and access to the mansion's lush gardens and outdoor patio. The bed and breakfast's central location puts guests within walking distance of Denver's top attractions, including the Colorado State Capitol, Denver Art Museum, and bustling dining and nightlife scene. Whether you're exploring the city's cultural landmarks or simply relaxing in the mansion's stately surroundings, Castle Marne Bed & Breakfast offers a memorable stay in the heart of Denver. Official website for booking and reservations: https://thecastlemarne.com/

Antlers on the Creek Bed & Breakfast
Escape to the picturesque town of Durango and discover the charm of Antlers on the Creek Bed & Breakfast, nestled along the banks of the tranquil Animas River. This intimate retreat offers cozy accommodations in a peaceful natural setting, with beautifully appointed rooms and suites featuring rustic décor and modern amenities. Prices for lodging at Antlers on the Creek vary depending on the season and room category, with rates typically ranging from $200 to $400 per night. Guests at Antlers on the Creek can enjoy a range of amenities, including a gourmet breakfast served each morning in the dining room or delivered to their room, complimentary afternoon wine and hors d'oeuvres, and access to the property's scenic gardens and riverside patio. The bed and breakfast's location provides the perfect base for exploring Durango's outdoor adventures, including hiking, biking, and river rafting, as well as its charming downtown area with its shops, galleries, and restaurants. Whether you're seeking

adventure in the great outdoors or simply seeking a peaceful retreat by the river, Antlers on the Creek Bed & Breakfast offers a warm and welcoming atmosphere for guests to relax and unwind. Official website for booking and reservations: https://antlersonthecreek.com/

The Dove Inn

Experience the charm of historic Golden with a stay at The Dove Inn, a beautifully restored Victorian-era bed and breakfast located in the heart of downtown. This boutique inn offers cozy accommodations in a charming setting, with individually decorated rooms featuring period furnishings and modern amenities. Prices for lodging at The Dove Inn vary depending on the season and room category, with rates typically ranging from $150 to $300 per night. Guests at The Dove Inn can enjoy a range of amenities, including a complimentary breakfast served each morning, access to a cozy library and parlor with board games and books, and complimentary snacks and beverages throughout the day. The inn's central location puts guests within walking distance of Golden's top attractions, including the Colorado School of Mines, Clear Creek History Park, and vibrant dining and shopping scene. Whether you're exploring the town's historic landmarks or simply relaxing on the inn's charming front porch, The Dove Inn offers a warm and inviting atmosphere for guests to enjoy a memorable stay in Golden. Official website for booking and reservations: https://www.doveinn.com/

2.4 Campgrounds and RV Parks

With its breathtaking landscapes and abundance of outdoor activities, Colorado is a paradise for camping enthusiasts and RV travelers alike. From rugged mountain vistas to serene lakeside retreats, the state offers a diverse array of campgrounds and RV parks for visitors to enjoy. These destinations provide the perfect opportunity to reconnect with nature and experience the beauty of the Rocky Mountains firsthand.

Rocky Mountain National Park Campgrounds

Situated amidst the awe-inspiring beauty of Rocky Mountain National Park, the park's campgrounds offer an unparalleled opportunity to immerse yourself in nature. With several campgrounds to choose from, including Moraine Park, Glacier Basin, and Aspenglen, visitors can enjoy a range of camping experiences, from wooded sites nestled among towering pine trees to open meadows with sweeping mountain views. Prices for camping in Rocky Mountain National Park vary depending on the campground and season, with rates typically ranging from $20 to $30 per night. Amenities at Rocky Mountain National Park campgrounds vary by location but often include picnic tables, fire rings, and access to restrooms and drinking water. Many campgrounds also offer ranger-led programs, hiking trails, and wildlife viewing opportunities. Whether you're pitching a tent or parking your RV, camping in Rocky Mountain National Park offers a memorable outdoor adventure surrounded by some of

Colorado's most iconic landscapes. Official website: https://www.rockymountainnationalpark.com/gallery/campgrounds/

Garden of the Gods RV Resort

Located just minutes from the iconic rock formations of Garden of the Gods in Colorado Springs, Garden of the Gods RV Resort offers a luxurious camping experience amidst stunning natural beauty. This top-rated RV resort features spacious RV sites with full hookups, as well as deluxe cabins and tent sites for those seeking a more traditional camping experience. Prices for lodging at Garden of the Gods RV Resort vary depending on the accommodation type and season, with rates typically ranging from $50 to $150 per night. Guests at Garden of the Gods RV Resort can enjoy a range of amenities, including a heated swimming pool, hot tub, fitness center, and dog park. The resort's prime location puts guests within easy reach of Garden of the Gods Park, as well as other popular attractions such as Pikes Peak and Manitou Springs. Whether you're exploring the area's natural wonders or simply relaxing at the resort, Garden of the Gods RV Resort offers a comfortable and convenient home base for your Colorado adventure. Website for booking and reservations: https://rvcoutdoors.com/garden-of-the-gods-rv-resort/

Lake Dillon Campgrounds

Nestled along the shores of scenic Lake Dillon in Summit County, Lake Dillon campgrounds offer a picturesque setting for outdoor enthusiasts to enjoy camping, fishing, boating, and hiking. The area boasts several campgrounds, including Prospector Campground, Heaton Bay Campground, and Peak One Campground, each offering its own unique charm and amenities. Prices for camping at Lake Dillon campgrounds vary depending on the campground and season, with rates typically ranging from $20 to $40 per night. Amenities at Lake Dillon campgrounds may include picnic tables, fire rings, and access to restrooms and drinking water. Many campgrounds also offer boat ramps, fishing piers, and hiking trails for guests to enjoy. With its stunning mountain views and abundance of outdoor activities, Lake Dillon is the perfect destination for a memorable camping getaway in Colorado's high country. Official website: https://www.dillonrangerdistrict.com/

Great Sand Dunes Oasis RV Park
Experience the unique beauty of Colorado's Great Sand Dunes National Park with a stay at the Great Sand Dunes Oasis RV Park. Located just minutes from the park entrance, this family-owned RV park offers spacious RV sites with full hookups, as well as tent sites and rental cabins for those seeking a more traditional camping experience. Prices for lodging at Great Sand Dunes Oasis RV Park vary depending on the accommodation type and season, with rates typically ranging from $30 to $70 per night. Guests at Great Sand Dunes Oasis RV Park can enjoy a range of amenities, including a heated swimming pool, hot tub, playground, and convenience store. The park's prime location puts guests within easy reach of the towering sand dunes of Great Sand

Dunes National Park, as well as other nearby attractions such as Zapata Falls and the town of Alamosa. Official website: https://greatdunes.com/

Mesa Verde RV Resort

Immerse yourself in the rich history and natural beauty of Mesa Verde National Park with a stay at Mesa Verde RV Resort. Located just minutes from the park entrance in Cortez, this modern RV resort offers spacious RV sites with full hookups, as well as tent sites and rental cabins for those seeking a more traditional camping experience. Prices for lodging at Mesa Verde RV Resort vary depending on the accommodation type and season, with rates typically ranging from $40 to $80 per night. Guests at Mesa Verde RV Resort can enjoy a range of amenities, including a swimming pool, hot tub, fitness center, and dog park. The resort's prime location puts guests within easy reach of Mesa Verde National Park's ancient cliff dwellings, as well as other nearby attractions such as the Four Corners Monument and the town of Durango. Whether you're exploring the park's archaeological sites or simply relaxing at the resort, Mesa Verde RV Resort offers a comfortable and convenient home base for your Colorado adventure. Official website: https://mesaverdervresort.com/

2.5 Unique Accommodation Experiences

Colorado is a land of diverse landscapes and unique experiences, and this extends to its accommodations. For travelers seeking something out of the ordinary, the state offers a variety of unconventional lodging options that promise unforgettable stays. From sleeping in a luxury treehouse to glamping in a yurt, these unique accommodation experiences in Colorado showcase the state's creativity and adventurous spirit.

Dunton Hot Springs

Tucked away in the rugged San Juan Mountains near Telluride, Dunton Hot Springs offers a truly unique accommodation experience in the form of luxurious cabins and a beautifully restored 19th-century ghost town. Prices for lodging at Dunton Hot Springs vary depending on the season and accommodation type, with rates typically ranging from $1000 to $3000 per night. Guests at Dunton Hot Springs can choose from a variety of accommodations, including handcrafted log cabins, cozy cottages, and even a restored miner's cabin. Each accommodation is beautifully appointed with rustic-chic decor and modern amenities, including plush bedding, private hot springs, and breathtaking views of the surrounding mountains. In addition to its luxurious accommodations, Dunton Hot Springs boasts a range of amenities and activities for guests to enjoy, including a world-class spa, gourmet dining experiences, and guided outdoor adventures such as hiking, horseback riding, and fly fishing. The resort's remote location and serene natural surroundings make it the perfect destination for those seeking a secluded and rejuvenating retreat in the heart of the Colorado wilderness. Website for booking and reservations: https://www.duntondestinations.com/hot-springs/

Treehouse Colorado

Perched among the towering pine trees of the Colorado Rockies, Treehouse Colorado offers a one-of-a-kind accommodation experience in the form of luxurious treehouse suites. Located near the charming mountain town of Golden, Treehouse Colorado provides guests with a unique blend of rustic charm and modern amenities. Prices for lodging at Treehouse Colorado vary depending on the season and accommodation type, with rates typically ranging from $300 to $600 per night. Each treehouse suite is elegantly furnished and features upscale amenities such as plush bedding, a private deck with stunning mountain views, and a cozy fireplace. Guests can also enjoy access to communal spaces, including a rooftop deck with a hot tub and a communal fire pit where they can gather under the stars. In addition to its unique accommodations, Treehouse Colorado offers a range of activities and experiences for guests to enjoy, including guided hikes, yoga classes, and gourmet dining experiences. Official website for booking and reservations: https://www.treehousehotsprings.com/

Royal Gorge Cabins

Nestled along the banks of the Arkansas River near Canon City, Royal Gorge Cabins offers a unique glamping experience that combines the comforts of home with the beauty of the great outdoors. Prices for lodging at Royal Gorge Cabins vary depending on the season and accommodation type, with rates typically ranging from $150 to $300 per night. Guests at Royal

Gorge Cabins can choose from a variety of accommodation options, including luxury tents and spacious cabins, each featuring stylish decor and modern amenities. The highlight of the resort is its riverside location, which provides guests with stunning views of the surrounding canyon walls and easy access to a variety of outdoor activities, including whitewater rafting, hiking, and rock climbing. In addition to its prime location and comfortable accommodations, Royal Gorge Cabins offers a range of amenities for guests to enjoy, including a heated swimming pool, hot tub, and onsite restaurant serving locally sourced cuisine. Whether you're seeking adventure on the river or relaxation by the fire, Royal Gorge Cabins offers a unique and unforgettable glamping experience in the heart of Colorado's wilderness. Website for booking and reservations: https://www.royalgorgecabins.com/

St. Elmo Hotel

Experience a taste of Colorado's rich history with a stay at the St. Elmo Hotel, a beautifully restored Victorian-era hotel located in the heart of downtown Ouray. Prices for lodging at the St. Elmo Hotel vary depending on the season and room type, with rates typically ranging from $100 to $300 per night. Built in 1898, the St. Elmo Hotel exudes old-world charm and elegance, with beautifully appointed guest rooms featuring period furnishings and modern amenities. Each room is uniquely decorated and offers guests a comfortable and inviting retreat after a day of exploring the surrounding area. In addition to its historic accommodations, the St. Elmo Hotel offers a range of amenities for guests to enjoy, including a complimentary breakfast served daily, access to a cozy parlor with a fireplace, and a rooftop hot tub with panoramic views of the surrounding mountains. Whether you're soaking in the hot tub under the stars or exploring the charming shops and restaurants of downtown Ouray, the St. Elmo Hotel offers a memorable and authentic Colorado experience. Website for booking and reservations: https://stelmohotel.com/

The Broadmoor Cloud Camp

Perched atop Cheyenne Mountain in Colorado Springs, The Broadmoor Cloud Camp offers a luxurious mountain retreat with breathtaking views of the surrounding landscape. Prices for lodging at The Broadmoor Cloud Camp vary depending on the season and accommodation type, with rates typically ranging from $800 to $2500 per night. Guests at The Broadmoor Cloud Camp can choose from a variety of accommodation options, including beautifully appointed lodge rooms and cozy cabins, each featuring rustic-chic decor and modern amenities. The highlight of the resort is its stunning mountaintop location, which provides guests with panoramic views of the surrounding mountains and easy access to a variety of outdoor activities, including hiking, mountain biking, and zip-lining. In addition to its luxurious accommodations, The Broadmoor Cloud Camp offers a range of amenities for guests to enjoy, including a gourmet restaurant serving locally sourced cuisine, a heated swimming pool, and a full-service spa. Official website for booking and reservations: https://www.broadmoor.com/cloud-camp

CHAPTER 3
TRANSPORTATION IN COLORADO

3.1 Public Transportation

Colorado, known for its stunning landscapes, vibrant cities, and outdoor recreational opportunities, offers a variety of public transportation options for both residents and visitors alike. From bustling metropolitan areas to serene mountain towns, the state boasts a network of transportation services designed to enhance mobility, reduce congestion, and promote sustainability. From efficient bus networks to light rail systems, Colorado's public transportation infrastructure ensures seamless connectivity across the state.

Public Transportation Services:

The Centennial State features a diverse array of public transportation services, catering to the needs of different communities and travelers. Among the prominent options are the Regional Transportation District (RTD) serving the Denver metropolitan area, the Bustang interregional bus service connecting major cities, and the Colorado Department of Transportation's (CDOT) Mountain Express service facilitating travel to mountain resorts.

Regional Transportation District (RTD):

The RTD serves as the primary public transit provider in the Denver metropolitan area, offering bus, light rail, and commuter rail services. Travelers can access an extensive network of routes covering Denver and its surrounding suburbs, including popular destinations such as Downtown Denver, Denver International Airport, and Red Rocks Park and Amphitheatre. The RTD's fare structure varies based on factors such as distance traveled, mode of transportation, and passenger demographics. Visitors can purchase tickets and passes through the RTD mobile app, ticket vending machines located at transit stations, or select retail outlets.

Bustang:

For interregional travel within Colorado, the Bustang bus service provides a convenient and affordable option. Operating several routes connecting major cities such as Denver, Colorado Springs, Fort Collins, and Grand Junction, Bustang offers comfortable coaches equipped with amenities such as Wi-Fi, restrooms, and bike racks. Fares are determined by route and distance, with discounts available for seniors, persons with disabilities, and children. Travelers can reserve seats in advance through the Bustang website or purchase tickets from the driver upon boarding.

Mountain Express:

Navigating the mountainous terrain of Colorado can be challenging, especially during winter months. To address this, CDOT operates the Mountain Express service, which facilitates transportation to popular ski resorts and recreational areas in the

Rocky Mountains. Whether heading to Aspen, Vail, Breckenridge, or other mountain destinations, visitors can rely on the Mountain Express for safe and reliable travel. Fares vary depending on the route and season, with options for single rides, round trips, and multi-day passes. Reservations are recommended, especially during peak travel periods, and can be made online or by phone.

Accessibility and Amenities:
Colorado's public transportation system prioritizes accessibility and passenger comfort, ensuring that individuals of all abilities can utilize the services with ease. Most transit vehicles are equipped with features such as wheelchair ramps, priority seating, and audio announcements to assist passengers with disabilities. Additionally, many transit stations and stops are designed to accommodate pedestrians and cyclists, with amenities such as bike racks, shelters, and information kiosks available for convenience.

3.2 Rental Cars and Car Sharing

Exploring the vast landscapes and diverse attractions of Colorado often necessitates reliable transportation, and for many visitors, renting a car or utilizing car-sharing services provides the freedom and flexibility to explore at their own pace. With a range of options available, from traditional car rental companies to innovative car-sharing platforms, travelers can easily access vehicles tailored to their needs and preferences, ensuring a seamless and memorable experience traversing the Centennial State's highways and byways.

Car Rental Companies:

Colorado boasts a plethora of car rental companies, offering an extensive selection of vehicles to suit various budgets and requirements. Among the prominent providers are national chains such as **Enterprise** (https://www.enterprise.com/), **Hertz** (https://www.hertz.com/), **Avis** (https://www.avis.com/), and **Budget** (https://www.budget.com/), which operate numerous rental locations throughout the state, including airports, downtown areas, and major tourist hubs. These established rental companies offer a diverse fleet comprising economy cars, SUVs, luxury vehicles, and specialty vehicles, ensuring options for every traveler's preferences and group size. Additionally, regional car rental agencies such as **Alamo Rent-A-Car** (https://www.alamo.com/) and **Thrifty Car Rental** (https://www.thrifty.com/) also serve customers in Colorado, providing competitive rates and personalized service. Whether arriving at Denver International Airport, exploring the scenic mountain towns of Aspen and Telluride, or embarking on a road trip through Rocky Mountain National Park, visitors can easily access rental vehicles from a variety of convenient locations across the state.

Prices and Booking:

Car rental prices in Colorado vary depending on factors such as vehicle type, rental duration, location, and seasonal demand. Generally, rates tend to be higher during peak travel periods, such as summer months and major holidays, while off-peak times may offer more competitive pricing. Travelers can compare prices and availability online through the websites of rental companies or third-party booking platforms, enabling them to secure the best deals and discounts in advance of their trip. Most car rental companies offer flexible booking options, allowing customers to reserve vehicles online, over the phone, or in person at rental locations. Rental agreements typically include provisions for insurance coverage, fuel policies, and mileage limits, so it's essential for visitors to review the terms and conditions carefully to ensure a smooth rental experience. Additionally, many rental agencies offer loyalty programs and promotional offers for frequent renters, providing opportunities for savings and additional perks.

Car Sharing Services:

In recent years, car-sharing services have emerged as a convenient and cost-effective alternative to traditional car rental. Platforms such as Turo (https://turo.com/), and Zipcar (https://www.zipcar.com/), allow users to rent vehicles directly from private owners or through a shared fleet, often providing more flexibility in terms of vehicle selection, pricing, and pickup locations. Car-sharing services are particularly popular in urban areas such as Denver, Boulder, and Colorado Springs, where access to public transportation may be limited, and short-term vehicle rentals are in high demand. To access car-sharing services in Colorado, travelers typically need to create an account on the respective platform's website or mobile app, where they can browse available vehicles, view pricing, and make reservations. Depending on the service provider, users may have the option to choose from a range of vehicle types, including compact cars, hybrids, and SUVs, with hourly or daily rental rates and mileage allowances. Many car-sharing companies also offer convenient pickup and drop-off locations, such as designated parking spots in downtown areas or near public transit stations.

Accessibility Options and Considerations:

When renting a car or utilizing car-sharing services in Colorado, visitors should consider factors such as insurance coverage, fuel efficiency, and driving conditions, especially when traveling in mountainous regions or during inclement weather. Additionally, it's important to familiarize oneself with local traffic laws, parking regulations, and road etiquette to ensure a safe and enjoyable driving experience. Furthermore, travelers with specific needs or preferences, such as child safety seats, GPS navigation systems, or winter tires, should communicate these requirements to rental companies or car-sharing hosts in advance to arrange for appropriate accommodations. By planning ahead and understanding the options available, visitors can make informed decisions when selecting a rental vehicle or car-sharing service that aligns with their travel plans and priorities.

3.3 Cycling and Bike Rentals

With its breathtaking scenery, extensive trail networks, and cyclist-friendly infrastructure, Colorado stands as a haven for cycling enthusiasts of all levels. From rugged mountain terrain to scenic urban pathways, the state offers a diverse range of cycling experiences that cater to both recreational riders and avid cyclists alike. For visitors looking to explore Colorado on two wheels, numerous bike rental companies provide convenient access to quality bicycles, ensuring an unforgettable journey through the Centennial State's picturesque landscapes.

Bike Rental Companies:

Colorado boasts an abundance of bike rental companies scattered throughout its various regions, each offering a unique selection of bicycles to suit different riding preferences and terrains. Among the renowned rental providers are shops such as Denver B-cycle (https://denver.bcycle.com/), which offers bike-sharing services in the Denver metropolitan area, allowing users to rent bicycles by the hour or through membership subscriptions. Similarly, companies like Wheel Fun Rentals (https://wheelfunrentals.com/) operate multiple locations across the state, offering a diverse fleet of bikes, including cruisers, mountain bikes, and tandem bicycles, ideal for exploring parks, trails, and urban areas. Additionally, specialty shops such as Absolute Bikes (https://www.absolutebikes.com/) in Salida and Durango Cyclery (https://www.durangocyclery.com/) in Durango cater to enthusiasts seeking high-performance road bikes, full-suspension mountain bikes, and bikepacking setups for extended adventures. These local bike shops often provide personalized service, expert advice, and maintenance support, ensuring that visitors have access to well-maintained and properly fitted bicycles for their excursions.

Prices and Booking:

Bike rental prices in Colorado vary depending on factors such as bike type, duration of rental, and location. Hourly rates for casual rentals typically range from $10 to $30, while full-day rentals may cost between $30 and $80, depending on the quality and specialty of the bike. Some rental companies also offer multi-day or weekly rental options, providing cost-effective solutions for visitors planning extended cycling trips or exploring multiple destinations. To access bike rental services in Colorado, visitors can typically make reservations online through the rental company's website or contact the rental shop directly to inquire about availability and pricing. Many rental companies offer convenient pickup and drop-off locations, including bike shops, hotels, and trailheads, allowing travelers to easily access their rental bicycles and begin their cycling adventures without hassle.

Trail Accessibility and Considerations:

Colorado's extensive network of cycling trails caters to riders of all skill levels, from beginners seeking leisurely rides along scenic pathways to experienced cyclists tackling challenging mountain terrain. Popular destinations such as the Colorado Front Range, Summit County, and the Western Slope offer a plethora of trails ranging from paved urban paths to rugged mountain singletracks, providing endless opportunities for exploration and adventure. Before hitting the trails, visitors should familiarize themselves with local trail regulations, etiquette, and safety guidelines to ensure a safe and enjoyable riding experience. Many trails in Colorado are multi-use and may be shared with hikers, runners, and equestrians, so cyclists should yield to other trail users and exercise caution, especially on narrow or congested sections. Furthermore, riders should be prepared for changing weather conditions, particularly in the mountains, where temperatures and precipitation can vary dramatically throughout the day. Packing essential gear such as water, snacks, layers of clothing, and a bike repair kit can help ensure preparedness for any unforeseen circumstances while out on the trail.

3.4 Taxi and Ride-Sharing Services

Navigating the vibrant streets and expansive landscapes of Colorado often requires convenient and reliable transportation options, and for many visitors, taxi and ride-sharing services provide the flexibility and accessibility needed to explore with ease. From bustling urban centers like Denver and Colorado Springs to remote mountain towns and resort areas, the Centennial State offers a variety of transportation solutions to suit every traveler's needs. With the emergence of ride-sharing platforms alongside traditional taxi services, visitors can choose from a range of options tailored to their preferences and budgets.

Taxi Services:

Traditional taxi services have long been a staple of urban transportation in Colorado, providing on-demand rides for passengers seeking point-to-point travel within cities and surrounding areas. Companies such as Yellow Cab, Metro Taxi, and Union Taxi operate fleets of licensed taxis equipped with meters, allowing passengers to pay based on distance traveled and time spent in the vehicle. Taxis can be hailed from designated taxi stands, called by phone, or booked through mobile apps, offering convenience and accessibility for travelers arriving at airports, train stations, and hotels.

Ride-Sharing Services:

In recent years, ride-sharing services have transformed the transportation landscape in Colorado, offering an alternative to traditional taxis with the convenience of smartphone-based booking and payment systems. Companies like **Uber** (https://www.uber.com/) and **Lyft** (https://www.lyft.com/) dominate the ride-sharing market, connecting passengers with drivers through user-friendly mobile apps. Riders can request rides, track their driver's location in real-time, and pay for their trip seamlessly through the app, eliminating the need for cash transactions and streamlining the overall experience.

Accessing Taxi and Ride-Sharing Services:

Accessing taxi and ride-sharing services in Colorado is simple and convenient, thanks to the widespread availability of smartphone technology and the prevalence of transportation apps. Travelers can download the Uber and Lyft apps from the App Store or Google Play Store and create accounts using their email address, phone number, and payment information. Once registered, users can input their pickup location and desired destination, select their preferred vehicle type (such as UberX, UberXL, Lyft Standard, or Lyft XL), and request a ride with just a few taps. Similarly, traditional taxi services can be accessed by calling local taxi dispatch numbers or using taxi-hailing apps where available. Many taxi companies also offer online booking options through their websites, allowing passengers to schedule rides in advance or request immediate pickups. Additionally, taxi stands can be found at major transportation hubs, hotels, and popular tourist destinations, providing a convenient option for travelers in need of quick and reliable transportation.

Prices and Fare Structure:

The pricing structure for taxi and ride-sharing services in Colorado varies depending on factors such as distance traveled, time of day, demand, and vehicle type. Ride-sharing companies like Uber and Lyft use dynamic pricing algorithms to adjust fares based on demand, with rates typically higher during peak hours, inclement weather, and special events. Conversely, taxi fares are regulated by local authorities and are based on a combination of a base fare, distance traveled, and waiting time. As a general guideline, taxi fares in Colorado start with a base rate of around $2.50 to $3.50, with additional charges of $2 to $3 per mile and $0.25 to $0.40 per minute of waiting time. Ride-sharing fares may vary more widely, but average rates for standard rides typically range from $1 to $2 per mile, with minimum fares and service fees applied. Both taxi and ride-sharing companies may also impose additional charges for factors such as airport pickups, tolls, and surge pricing during periods of high demand.

Accessibility and Considerations:
When utilizing ride-sharing services in Colorado, travelers should consider factors such as accessibility, safety, and convenience. Most ride-sharing vehicles are equipped to accommodate passengers with disabilities, with options for wheelchair-accessible vehicles available upon request. Additionally, riders should ensure that they are entering the correct pickup location and verifying the driver's identity and vehicle information provided through the app for added safety and security. Furthermore, riders should be aware of local regulations and guidelines regarding ride-sharing services, including designated pickup and drop-off zones, parking restrictions, and surge pricing during peak demand periods. By staying informed and exercising caution when using ride-sharing services, travelers can enjoy a convenient and hassle-free transportation experience while exploring the sights and attractions of Colorado.

3.5 Driving Tips and Road Conditions

Embarking on a road trip through Colorado offers travelers an unparalleled opportunity to witness the state's breathtaking landscapes, from towering mountain peaks to sprawling plains and picturesque valleys. However, navigating Colorado's diverse terrain and ever-changing weather conditions requires careful preparation and awareness of driving tips and road conditions.

From mountain passes to urban highways, understanding the nuances of driving in Colorado can enhance safety, enjoyment, and overall travel experience for visitors exploring the Centennial State.

Driving Tips:
Driving in Colorado presents unique challenges and considerations due to its varied topography, elevation changes, and weather patterns. To ensure a smooth and safe journey, visitors should adhere to the following driving tips:

Weather Awareness: Colorado's weather can be unpredictable, especially in mountainous regions. Be prepared for sudden changes in weather conditions, including snowstorms, heavy rain, and high winds, particularly during winter months and at higher elevations.

Altitude Adjustment: Many areas of Colorado are located at high altitudes, which can affect both drivers and vehicles. Take breaks to acclimate to the altitude, stay hydrated, and be mindful of symptoms of altitude sickness, such as headache, nausea, and dizziness.

Mountain Driving: When traversing mountain passes and steep grades, exercise caution and use lower gears to control speed and reduce strain on brakes. Be aware of wildlife, sharp curves, and narrow roads, and yield to uphill traffic when possible.

Road Etiquette: Follow traffic laws and posted speed limits, and be courteous to other drivers, cyclists, and pedestrians. Use turn signals, maintain a safe following distance, and yield to emergency vehicles and construction zones.

Emergency Preparedness: Carry essentials such as water, snacks, a first-aid kit, flashlight, and blankets in case of emergencies. Keep a fully charged phone and know how to access roadside assistance services in case of breakdowns or accidents.

Road Conditions:

Road conditions in Colorado exhibit considerable diversity, influenced by factors such as geography, elevation, weather patterns, and human activity. The state's mountainous terrain presents unique challenges, particularly in winter, when mountain passes can become treacherous due to heavy snowfall, icy conditions, and reduced visibility. Popular passes like Loveland Pass and Independence Pass require drivers to exercise caution, use proper snow equipment, and check for road closures before attempting to traverse them. Visitors can check road conditions and closures in real-time through the Colorado Department of Transportation (CDOT) website or by calling the Colorado Road Conditions hotline. In contrast, urban areas in Colorado generally boast well-maintained roads, but they are not immune to challenges. Traffic congestion, construction zones, and accidents can impact travel times and road safety, requiring drivers to remain vigilant and adapt to changing conditions. Moreover, rural roads and backcountry routes offer scenic drives but may lack regular maintenance, leading to hazards such as potholes, debris, and wildlife crossings. Navigating these routes demands attentiveness, moderate speeds, and an awareness of surroundings.

Weather plays a significant role in shaping road conditions throughout Colorado, with winter presenting the most significant challenges. Snowstorms, freezing rain, and high winds can create hazardous driving conditions, prompting road closures and travel restrictions. Drivers must be prepared for sudden weather changes, equip their vehicles with appropriate gear like snow tires and chains, and heed weather advisories to ensure safe travel. Additionally, considerations like cell phone coverage, emergency services availability, and access to amenities vary across different regions of the state. In remote areas, drivers may encounter limited cell phone reception and longer response times for emergency assistance, underscoring the importance of preparedness and self-sufficiency.

Overall, navigating Colorado's roads requires a blend of caution, preparedness, and adaptability. By staying informed about road conditions, practicing defensive driving techniques, and respecting local regulations and guidelines, motorists can enjoy a safe and rewarding journey through the diverse landscapes of the Centennial State.

CHAPTER 4
TOP ATTRACTIONS/HIDDEN GEMS

Click the link or Scan QR Code with a device to view a comprehensive map of Top Attractions in Colorado –
https://shorturl.at/jkxFO

4.1 Must-Visit Landmarks

Colorado, with its stunning natural beauty and rich cultural heritage, is home to a plethora of must-visit landmarks that captivate the imagination and inspire awe in visitors from around the world. From towering peaks to ancient cliff dwellings, each landmark offers a unique glimpse into the state's diverse landscapes and storied history. Exploring these iconic sites promises an unforgettable journey filled with adventure, discovery, and wonder.

Rocky Mountain National Park:
Nestled in the heart of the Rocky Mountains, Rocky Mountain National Park stands as a testament to the grandeur of nature. With its soaring peaks, pristine alpine lakes, and verdant forests, the park offers endless opportunities for outdoor recreation and exploration. Visitors can hike along scenic trails, marvel at cascading waterfalls, and spot diverse wildlife, including elk, bighorn sheep, and black bears. Trail Ridge Road, known as the "highway to the sky," offers breathtaking views of the surrounding mountains and valleys, while the historic town of Estes Park provides charming accommodations and amenities for travelers.

Mesa Verde National Park:
For a glimpse into the ancient past, Mesa Verde National Park beckons with its remarkable archaeological sites and cliff dwellings built by the ancestral Puebloans over 700 years ago. Perched atop steep cliffs and nestled within sandstone alcoves, these well-preserved dwellings offer a fascinating glimpse into the lives of the people who once called this region home. Visitors can explore the park's numerous cliff dwellings, including the iconic Cliff Palace and Balcony House, marveling at the intricate stone

masonry and ingenious architectural techniques used by the ancient inhabitants. Guided tours and interpretive programs provide insight into the culture and history of the ancestral Puebloans, making Mesa Verde a must-visit destination for history enthusiasts and nature lovers alike.

Garden of the Gods:

Located near the city of Colorado Springs, Garden of the Gods is a geological marvel renowned for its towering sandstone rock formations and stunning natural beauty. Carved by the forces of wind and water over millions of years, these red rock spires and rock formations create a surreal landscape that is both captivating and awe-inspiring. Visitors can explore the park's numerous hiking trails, rock climbing routes, and scenic overlooks, immersing themselves in the unique geology and diverse plant and animal life of the area. The Visitor Center offers interpretive exhibits, guided nature walks, and educational programs, providing insights into the park's natural and cultural history.

Pikes Peak:

Rising majestically above the Colorado landscape, Pikes Peak is one of the most iconic mountains in the state, offering panoramic views of the surrounding plains and mountains from its summit. Accessible via the Pikes Peak Highway or the historic cog railway, the mountain beckons adventure seekers and outdoor enthusiasts to embark on a journey to its 14,115-foot peak. Along the way, visitors can marvel at cascading waterfalls, alpine meadows, and rugged rock formations, pausing to catch their breath and take in the breathtaking vistas. At the summit, the Summit House offers refreshments, souvenirs, and unparalleled views stretching as far as the eye can see, making Pikes Peak a must-visit destination for nature lovers and thrill-seekers alike.

Great Sand Dunes National Park and Preserve:
Tucked away in the southern reaches of Colorado, Great Sand Dunes National Park and Preserve is a surreal landscape of towering sand dunes, rolling grasslands, and snow-capped peaks. Home to the tallest sand dunes in North America, the park offers endless opportunities for exploration and adventure. Visitors can hike among the dunes, sandboard or sled down their slopes, or splash in the seasonal Medano Creek, creating unforgettable memories amidst this unique natural playground. The park's diverse ecosystems support a wide variety of plant and animal life, from desert-adapted species to alpine flora and fauna, making it a haven for nature lovers and photographers.

4.2 Off-The-Beaten-Path Destinations

While Colorado is known for its iconic landmarks and popular tourist destinations, the state also boasts a wealth of hidden gems and off-the-beaten-path destinations waiting to be discovered. From secluded mountain lakes to ghost towns frozen in time, these lesser-known treasures offer intrepid travelers a chance to escape the crowds and immerse themselves in the natural beauty and rich history of the Centennial State. Exploring these hidden gems promises a journey of discovery, adventure, and unforgettable experiences for those willing to venture off the well-trodden path.

Maroon Bells Wilderness:

Tucked away in the heart of the Elk Mountains, the Maroon Bells-Snowmass Wilderness is a pristine wilderness area renowned for its rugged peaks, alpine meadows, and crystalline lakes. Accessible from the town of Aspen, this remote wilderness offers a myriad of hiking trails ranging from easy day hikes to challenging multi-day backpacking adventures. The iconic Maroon Bells, two towering peaks reflected in the tranquil waters of Maroon Lake, provide a stunning backdrop for outdoor enthusiasts seeking solitude and serenity amidst Colorado's stunning landscapes. Visitors can explore the area's diverse ecosystems, spot wildlife such as elk and mule deer, and camp beneath a canopy of stars in designated backcountry campsites.

Black Canyon of the Gunnison National Park:

Hidden away in the rugged terrain of western Colorado, the Black Canyon of the Gunnison National Park is a dramatic landscape of sheer cliffs, deep gorges, and roaring rapids carved by the mighty Gunnison River. Often overshadowed by its more famous counterparts, this lesser-known gem offers visitors a chance to experience the raw power and beauty of nature in a secluded and uncrowded setting. Hiking trails lead to breathtaking overlooks, where visitors can peer into the depths of the canyon and marvel at its sheer walls plunging thousands of feet to the river below. For adventurous souls, rock climbing and whitewater rafting opportunities await, providing adrenaline-pumping thrills amidst the park's rugged terrain.

Great Sand Dunes National Preserve:
Nestled in the shadow of the Sangre de Cristo Mountains in southern Colorado, the Great Sand Dunes National Preserve is a surreal landscape of towering sand dunes, rolling grasslands, and shimmering streams. While the adjacent Great Sand Dunes National Park draws crowds with its iconic dunes and recreational activities, the preserve offers a quieter and more secluded experience for intrepid travelers. Visitors can hike among the dunes, following ephemeral streams and discovering hidden pockets of lush vegetation teeming with life. Birdwatchers will delight in the preserve's diverse avian species, while stargazers can marvel at the Milky Way stretching across the night sky, undimmed by city lights.

Crystal Mill:
Tucked away in the rugged mountains near Marble, Colorado, the Crystal Mill stands as a relic of the state's mining past, frozen in time amidst the stunning beauty of the Crystal River Valley. Accessible via a rugged four-wheel-drive road or a scenic hike along the Crystal River, this historic mill offers a glimpse into Colorado's rich mining heritage and the challenges faced by early settlers in the region. Perched precariously on the edge of a

cascading waterfall, the mill's weathered wooden frame and rusting machinery evoke a sense of nostalgia and adventure, transporting visitors back to a bygone era of frontier life. Photographers and history enthusiasts alike will find inspiration in the mill's picturesque setting and timeless allure.

Great Sand Dunes Oasis:

Tucked away in the shadow of the towering sand dunes of Great Sand Dunes National Park, the Great Sand Dunes Oasis offers a unique and off-the-beaten-path lodging experience for travelers seeking adventure and relaxation amidst Colorado's natural beauty. Situated along the banks of the scenic Sand Creek, this rustic oasis features cozy cabins, tent sites, and RV hookups, providing a comfortable basecamp for exploring the surrounding dunes and wilderness. Visitors can relax in the natural hot springs, soak up the sunshine on the sandy beaches, or embark on guided tours of the park's iconic dunes and diverse ecosystems. With its secluded location and stunning views of the surrounding mountains, Great Sand Dunes Oasis offers a peaceful retreat from the hustle and bustle of everyday life, inviting travelers to reconnect with nature and create lasting memories amidst Colorado's pristine landscapes.

4.3 Scenic Drives and Byways

Colorado's scenic drives and byways wind through some of the most breathtaking landscapes in the United States, offering visitors a chance to experience the state's natural beauty up close. From rugged mountain passes to sweeping prairies, these routes traverse a diverse tapestry of terrain, providing travelers with panoramic views, charming towns, and opportunities for outdoor adventure. Exploring these scenic drives promises an unforgettable journey filled with awe-inspiring vistas, hidden gems, and memorable experiences for those seeking to immerse themselves in the splendor of the Centennial State.

Trail Ridge Road:
Widely acclaimed as one of the most scenic drives in the United States, Trail Ridge Road traverses the heart of Rocky Mountain National Park, offering unrivaled views of the park's towering peaks, alpine meadows, and pristine lakes. Stretching for 48 miles between the towns of Estes Park and Grand Lake, this high-altitude highway climbs to an elevation of over 12,000 feet, making it the highest continuous paved road in North America. Along the way, visitors can marvel at the park's diverse ecosystems, spot wildlife such as elk and bighorn sheep, and stop at scenic overlooks to capture panoramic views of the surrounding mountains and valleys. Trail Ridge Road is typically open from late spring to early fall, offering a window of opportunity for travelers to experience this iconic drive at its most spectacular.

Million Dollar Highway:
Named for its stunning scenery and rumored cost of construction, the Million Dollar Highway winds its way through the rugged terrain of the San Juan Mountains in southwestern Colorado, connecting

the historic mining towns of Durango and Ouray. The highway's narrow lanes, steep grades, and hairpin turns offer a thrilling driving experience, with jaw-dropping views of towering peaks, deep canyons, and cascading waterfalls at every turn. Along the route, travelers can explore historic mining towns, soak in natural hot springs, and embark on outdoor adventures such as hiking, fishing, and rock climbing. While the drive can be challenging, especially in winter, the breathtaking scenery and sense of adventure make it a must-do for intrepid travelers seeking to experience Colorado's wild side.

Peak to Peak Scenic Byway:
Stretching for 55 miles through the Front Range of the Rocky Mountains, the Peak to Peak Scenic Byway offers a leisurely journey through some of Colorado's most picturesque landscapes, from alpine forests to rolling meadows. Beginning in the historic mining town of Central City and ending in Estes Park, the byway passes through charming mountain communities, historic sites, and scenic overlooks, providing ample opportunities for exploration and discovery. Along the route, visitors can hike to hidden waterfalls, admire colorful wildflowers in summer, and spot wildlife such as moose, deer, and black bears. The byway is particularly popular in the fall when the aspen trees turn vibrant shades of gold and orange, creating a stunning backdrop for a scenic drive.

Independence Pass:

Ascending to an elevation of over 12,000 feet, Independence Pass offers travelers a breathtaking journey through the heart of the Sawatch Range in central Colorado. Beginning in the town of Twin Lakes and winding its way through the White River National Forest, the pass traverses rugged terrain, alpine meadows, and dense forests, providing stunning views of snow-capped peaks and crystal-clear mountain lakes. Along the route, visitors can explore historic sites such as the ghost town of Independence, marvel at the power of cascading waterfalls, and embark on outdoor adventures such as hiking, fishing, and wildlife watching. While the pass is typically open from late spring to early fall, it can be subject to closures during inclement weather, so travelers should check road conditions before embarking on their journey.

San Juan Skyway:

Widely regarded as one of the most scenic drives in the United States, the San Juan Skyway takes travelers on a spectacular journey through the rugged landscapes of southwestern Colorado, encompassing towering peaks, deep canyons, and historic mining towns. Beginning in the city of Durango, the 233-mile loop route passes through iconic destinations such as Silverton, Ouray, and Telluride, offering stunning views of the region's diverse scenery and cultural heritage. Along the way, visitors can explore historic mining sites, soak in natural hot springs, and indulge in outdoor activities such as hiking, mountain biking, and horseback riding. The drive is particularly breathtaking in the fall when the aspen trees transform the landscape into a patchwork of vibrant colors, creating a photographer's paradise.

4.4 Local Festivals and Events

Colorado's vibrant culture and diverse communities come alive throughout the year with a myriad of local festivals and events that celebrate everything from music and art to food and heritage. These gatherings offer visitors a unique opportunity to immerse themselves in the spirit of Colorado, experiencing the state's rich traditions, flavors, and creativity firsthand. From lively music festivals to colorful cultural celebrations, each event provides a window into the heart and soul of the Centennial State, inviting travelers to join in the festivities and create unforgettable memories.

Telluride Bluegrass Festival:

Nestled in the picturesque town of Telluride amidst the rugged peaks of the San Juan Mountains, the Telluride Bluegrass Festival is a celebration of music, community, and mountain culture. Held annually in June, this iconic festival draws thousands of music lovers from around the world to revel in four days of live performances by some of the biggest names in bluegrass, folk, and Americana music. From intimate acoustic sets to raucous jam sessions, the festival's diverse lineup offers something for every musical taste, while its stunning mountain setting provides a breathtaking backdrop for unforgettable performances. In addition to the main stage concerts, attendees can participate in workshops, jam sessions, and late-night concerts, immersing themselves in the vibrant spirit of Telluride's music scene.

Colorado Dragon Boat Festival:

Held annually at Sloan's Lake Park in Denver, the Colorado Dragon Boat Festival is a vibrant celebration of Asian culture and heritage that attracts thousands of visitors each year. Featuring colorful dragon boat races, traditional dance performances, martial arts demonstrations, and a bustling marketplace showcasing Asian cuisine and crafts, the festival offers a feast for the senses and a glimpse into the rich tapestry of Asian American communities in Colorado. Visitors can cheer on teams of paddlers as they compete in dragon boat races on the lake, sample delicious Asian cuisine from food vendors, and browse a diverse array of arts and crafts from local artisans. With its lively atmosphere and family-friendly activities, the Colorado Dragon Boat Festival is a must-visit event for anyone interested in experiencing the vibrant cultural diversity of the Centennial State.

Great American Beer Festival:

As the largest beer festival and competition in the United States, the Great American Beer Festival in Denver is a mecca for beer enthusiasts and craft brewers alike. Held annually in October at the Colorado Convention Center, the festival features over 4,000 different beers from more than 800 breweries across the country, providing attendees with a unique opportunity to sample a vast array of craft beers and discover new favorites. In addition to the beer tasting sessions, the festival also offers educational seminars, brewery tours, and interactive exhibits where visitors can learn about the brewing process and meet the brewers behind their favorite beers. With its lively atmosphere, live music, and festive spirit, the Great American Beer Festival is a beer lover's paradise and a must-visit event for anyone passionate about craft beer and brewing culture.

Boulder International Film Festival:

Celebrating the art of cinema and independent filmmaking, the Boulder International Film Festival (BIFF) showcases a diverse selection of narrative and documentary films from around the world. Held annually in February in the charming college town of Boulder, BIFF attracts filmmakers, industry professionals, and cinephiles alike to participate in screenings, panel discussions, and special events celebrating the power of storytelling through film. Attendees can enjoy a wide variety of screenings, including feature films, shorts, and documentaries, as well as filmmaker Q&A sessions and special presentations. With its vibrant film community, picturesque setting, and eclectic lineup of films, the Boulder International Film Festival offers a unique and memorable cinematic experience for movie lovers of all ages.

Colorado Renaissance Festival:

Step back in time to the days of knights, jesters, and fair maidens at the Colorado Renaissance Festival, a beloved summer tradition held annually in Larkspur, just south of Denver. Spanning eight weekends from June to August, this enchanting festival transports visitors to a medieval village filled with artisans, performers, and costumed characters who bring the Renaissance era to life. Attendees can wander through the village streets, browsing handcrafted goods, sampling hearty fare, and enjoying live entertainment ranging from jousting tournaments and stage performances to music, comedy, and interactive demonstrations. With its festive atmosphere, elaborate costumes, and immersive historical setting, the Colorado Renaissance Festival offers a magical escape for visitors of all ages, inviting them to experience the magic and wonder of the Renaissance era firsthand.

4.5 Unique Experiences and Activities

Colorado offers visitors a wealth of unique experiences and activities that showcase the state's natural beauty, adventurous spirit, and rich cultural heritage. From exploring ancient cliff dwellings to soaring high above the Rocky Mountains in a hot air balloon, these one-of-a-kind experiences promise unforgettable memories and a deeper connection to the diverse landscapes and vibrant communities of the Centennial State. Whether seeking outdoor adventure, cultural immersion, or simply a chance to unwind amidst stunning scenery, Colorado offers something special for every traveler.

Hot Air Balloon Ride Over the Rockies:
Soar high above the majestic peaks of the Rocky Mountains on a hot air balloon ride, offering a bird's-eye view of Colorado's

stunning landscapes and dramatic vistas. Drifting serenely through the crisp mountain air, passengers are treated to panoramic views of snow-capped peaks, alpine lakes, and lush valleys stretching as far as the eye can see. As the sun rises or sets, casting a warm glow over the mountains, the experience becomes truly magical, offering a sense of peace and tranquility that can only be found high above the earth. Several companies in Colorado offer hot air balloon rides, with launch sites located throughout the state, including Boulder, Colorado Springs, and the Vail Valley, providing travelers with ample opportunities to take to the skies and experience the beauty of Colorado from a whole new perspective.

Glenwood Caverns Adventure Park Cave Tours:
Descend into the depths of the earth and explore the fascinating underground world of Glenwood Caverns Adventure Park, home to some of the most extensive cave systems in Colorado. Guided cave tours offer visitors a chance to marvel at intricate stalactites, stalagmites, and other geological formations, as well as learn about the park's rich history and unique ecosystem. Highlights of the tour include the Fairy Caves, King's Row, and the Historic Fairy Caves, where visitors can experience the awe-inspiring beauty and natural wonders of these subterranean caverns. In addition to cave tours, the adventure park offers a variety of thrill rides, attractions, and activities for visitors of all ages, making it a must-visit destination for families, adventure seekers, and nature lovers alike.

Dinosaur Ridge:

Step back in time to the age of the dinosaurs at Dinosaur Ridge, a world-renowned paleontological site located just west of Denver in Morrison, Colorado. This outdoor museum offers visitors a chance to walk in the footsteps of giants as they explore ancient dinosaur tracks, fossils, and rock formations dating back over 150 million years. Guided tours led by knowledgeable interpreters provide insights into the park's rich history and the fascinating creatures that once roamed the area, including the mighty Tyrannosaurus rex and the iconic Stegosaurus. Visitors can also explore the park's hiking trails, picnic areas, and visitor center, immersing themselves in the natural beauty and prehistoric wonders of Dinosaur Ridge.

Train Rides Through the Royal Gorge:

Embark on a scenic journey through one of Colorado's most spectacular natural wonders aboard the Royal Gorge Route Railroad, offering passengers a front-row seat to breathtaking views of the Royal Gorge Canyon. Departing from Cañon City, Colorado, the historic train follows a route along the Arkansas River, winding through rugged cliffs, towering rock formations, and sheer granite walls towering over 1,000 feet high. As the train traverses the canyon, passengers can relax in vintage railcars, enjoy gourmet cuisine and cocktails in the dining car, and soak in the awe-inspiring scenery from open-air observation platforms. Knowledgeable tour guides also provide commentary on the area, enhancing the experience and providing insight into the natural wonders of the Royal Gorge.

Skiing and Snowboarding in the Rockies:

Experience the thrill of gliding down powdery slopes and carving fresh tracks through pristine snow at one of Colorado's world-class ski resorts. With over 25 ski areas scattered throughout the state, including iconic destinations such as Aspen, Vail, and Breckenridge, Colorado offers some of the best skiing and snowboarding in North America. From gentle beginner slopes to challenging expert terrain, there's something for every skill level and interest, making it an ideal destination for winter sports enthusiasts of all ages. In addition to skiing and snowboarding, many resorts offer a variety of other winter activities, including snowshoeing, snowmobiling, and ice skating, providing visitors with endless opportunities for outdoor adventure and excitement amidst the stunning beauty of the Rocky Mountains.

CHAPTER 5

PRACTICAL INFORMATION AND TRAVEL RESOURCES

5.1 Maps and Navigation

Click the link or Scan the QR Code with a device to view a comprehensive map of Colorado – https://shorturl.at/gnMS5

Colorado, a land of majestic mountains, sprawling plains, and vibrant cities, beckons travelers with its breathtaking landscapes and rich cultural heritage. As you embark on your journey through this diverse state, navigating its vast terrain becomes paramount.

Colorado Tourist Map:

A trusty companion for any traveler venturing into the heart of Colorado is the Colorado Tourist Map. Available at visitor centers, airports, and various tourist hubs across the state, this map offers a comprehensive overview of Colorado's highways, scenic routes, national parks, and points of interest. Illustrated with vibrant colors and detailed landmarks, it serves as a visual guide to help you chart your course through the wonders of Colorado.

Accessing Offline Maps: For those who prefer the reliability of paper maps, accessing offline maps in Colorado is a breeze. Local convenience stores, gas stations, and bookshops often carry a variety of maps tailored to specific regions or interests within the state. Additionally, visitor centers and tourism offices are excellent resources for procuring free or inexpensive maps, complete with insider tips and local recommendations.

Digital Maps:

In an age of technological innovation, digital maps have revolutionized the way we navigate unfamiliar terrain. Colorado boasts a plethora of digital mapping services, ranging from popular applications like **Google Maps** (https://maps.google.com/) and **Apple Maps** (https://www.apple.com/maps/) to specialized platforms such as **AllTrails** (https://www.alltrails.com/) and **Gaia GPS** (https://www.gaiagps.com/). These digital tools offer real-time navigation, interactive features, and customizable routes, making them invaluable companions for modern-day explorers.

Accessing Digital Maps:

Accessing Colorado's digital maps is a seamless process, thanks to the widespread availability of internet connectivity and mobile devices. Whether you're exploring the bustling streets of Denver or traversing the rugged trails of Rocky Mountain National Park, a smartphone or tablet equipped with a reliable data connection allows you to access digital maps on the go. Additionally, many mapping applications offer offline functionality, enabling you to download maps for offline use in areas with limited connectivity.

Comprehensive Map of Colorado:

As an added convenience for readers and travelers, this guide provides access to a comprehensive map of Colorado via a clickable link or QR code. This digital map offers an immersive experience, allowing users to zoom in on specific regions, discover hidden gems, and plan their adventures with ease. Whether you're seeking scenic drives, hiking trails, or historical landmarks, this interactive map serves as a virtual gateway to the wonders of Colorado.

Additional Information:

Beyond maps and navigation, there are several important considerations for visitors exploring Colorado. Be sure to familiarize yourself with local regulations and safety guidelines, especially when venturing into remote wilderness areas. Weather conditions in Colorado can vary dramatically depending on the season and elevation, so pack accordingly and check forecasts regularly. Lastly, embrace the spirit of adventure and immerse yourself in the rich tapestry of experiences that Colorado has to offer.

5.2 Essential Packing List

Preparing for a visit to Colorado requires careful consideration of the diverse terrain and fluctuating weather conditions that characterize this enchanting state. From the towering peaks of the Rocky Mountains to the bustling streets of its vibrant cities, Colorado offers a myriad of experiences for travelers. In this guide, we outline an essential packing list to ensure you're equipped for whatever adventures await.

Clothing:
Colorado's weather can be unpredictable, with temperature variations depending on elevation and time of year. It's essential to pack versatile clothing suitable for layering. Be sure to include moisture-wicking base layers, insulating mid-layers, and a waterproof outer shell to stay comfortable in changing conditions. Additionally, pack sturdy hiking boots for exploring trails and comfortable walking shoes for urban adventures. Don't forget to include hats, gloves, and scarves for added warmth during chilly evenings or high-altitude excursions.

Outdoor Gear:
For outdoor enthusiasts, Colorado offers a playground of recreational activities, from hiking and skiing to camping and rock climbing. Depending on your interests, pack essential outdoor gear such as a backpack, water bottles or hydration reservoirs, sunscreen, sunglasses, and a wide-brimmed hat for sun protection. If you plan to hike or camp in remote areas, consider bringing a map, compass or GPS device, first aid kit, and emergency supplies such as a whistle, flashlight, and extra food and water.

Travel Accessories:

When traveling to Colorado, certain accessories can enhance your experience and ensure smooth transitions between destinations. Consider packing a sturdy travel backpack or duffel bag for carrying essentials during day trips or excursions. A portable charger or power bank is handy for keeping your devices charged while on the go, especially if you'll be using digital maps or navigating unfamiliar terrain. Don't forget to pack any necessary travel documents, including identification, insurance cards, and reservation confirmations.

Health and Safety Essentials:

Maintaining your health and safety is paramount while traveling, especially in remote or wilderness areas. Pack any prescription medications, as well as over-the-counter remedies for common ailments such as headaches, allergies, and upset stomachs. It's also wise to include a basic first aid kit with bandages, antiseptic wipes, and pain relievers. If you're exploring at high altitudes, be mindful of symptoms of altitude sickness and take precautions such as staying hydrated and acclimatizing gradually.

Electronics and Gadgets:

In today's digital age, electronics and gadgets are indispensable travel companions for capturing memories, staying connected, and navigating unfamiliar terrain. Pack a reliable camera or smartphone for capturing photos and videos of Colorado's stunning landscapes and attractions. Consider bringing a portable

GPS device or downloading offline maps for navigating remote areas where cellular coverage may be limited. Additionally, pack any necessary chargers, adapters, and accessories for your electronic devices.

As you prepare for your visit to Colorado, remember that proper packing is key to a comfortable and enjoyable experience. By including essential clothing, outdoor gear, travel accessories, health and safety essentials, and electronics and gadgets, you'll be well-equipped to embrace the adventures that await in the Centennial State.

5.3 Visa Requirements and Entry Procedures

Planning a visit to Colorado involves not only preparing for the adventures that await within the state but also ensuring compliance with visa requirements and entry procedures. Whether you're traveling for leisure, business, or other purposes, understanding the necessary documentation and procedures is essential for a smooth and hassle-free journey.

Visa Requirements:

The United States, including Colorado, has specific visa requirements for visitors from foreign countries. The type of visa you need depends on factors such as your country of citizenship, the purpose of your visit, and the duration of your stay. For most travelers visiting Colorado for tourism or business purposes, the B-1/B-2 visitor visa is appropriate. This visa allows for temporary visits to the United States for tourism, business meetings, or medical treatment. It's important to apply for the appropriate visa well in advance of your planned travel dates and to carefully follow the application instructions provided by the U.S. Department of State.

Electronic System for Travel Authorization (ESTA):
For citizens of certain countries participating in the Visa Waiver Program (VWP), the Electronic System for Travel Authorization (ESTA) may be an alternative to obtaining a traditional visa. ESTA allows eligible travelers to enter the United States for short-term visits (typically 90 days or less) without a visa for purposes of tourism, business, or transit. However, travelers must apply for ESTA authorization online through the official website of the U.S. Customs and Border Protection (CBP) at least 72 hours before their departure. It's important to note that ESTA authorization does not guarantee entry into the United States and is subject to approval by CBP.

Entry Procedures:
Upon arrival in the United States, travelers to Colorado will go through immigration and customs procedures at their port of entry. Be prepared to present your passport, visa (if required), and any supporting documentation to the immigration officer. It's essential to answer questions truthfully and accurately, as providing false information could result in denial of entry or other legal consequences. Additionally, customs regulations apply to certain

items you may be bringing into the country, such as food, plants, and merchandise for resale. Familiarize yourself with these regulations to avoid delays or confiscation of prohibited items.

Travel Authorization:

In addition to a valid visa or ESTA authorization, travelers to Colorado must ensure they have the necessary travel authorization documents before boarding their flight. This includes a valid passport with an expiration date that meets the requirements of the U.S. Department of Homeland Security (DHS). It's recommended to review your passport's expiration date and renew it if necessary well in advance of your planned travel dates. Some airlines may also require travelers to provide proof of onward travel or a return ticket before allowing them to board the aircraft.

5.4 Safety Tips and Emergency Contacts

While Colorado offers boundless opportunities for exploration and adventure, it's essential for visitors to prioritize safety during their travels. From outdoor activities in the rugged wilderness to navigating bustling urban environments, understanding safety tips and emergency contacts is crucial for a worry-free experience in the Centennial State.

Outdoor Safety:

For those venturing into Colorado's vast natural landscapes, it's vital to be prepared for the challenges and potential hazards of outdoor activities. Before embarking on hikes, camping trips, or other adventures, research your chosen destination and familiarize yourself with the terrain, weather conditions, and any potential risks such as wildlife encounters or avalanches. Always carry essential safety gear, including a map, compass or GPS device, first aid kit, extra food and water, and appropriate clothing and footwear for the environment. Additionally, inform someone of your itinerary and expected return time before heading out, and never underestimate the importance of staying hydrated, avoiding overexertion, and respecting local regulations and guidelines.

Weather Preparedness:
Colorado's weather can be unpredictable, with rapid changes in temperature and conditions, especially in mountainous regions. Whether you're hiking, skiing, or exploring urban areas, it's essential to stay informed about current weather forecasts and be prepared for sudden shifts in weather patterns. Dress in layers to adjust to changing temperatures, and always carry rain gear or a waterproof jacket in case of inclement weather. If you're traveling during the winter months, be aware of the risks associated with snowstorms, icy roads, and avalanches, and exercise caution when driving or participating in winter sports activities.

Urban Safety:
Even in Colorado's vibrant cities and towns, it's important to remain vigilant and take precautions to ensure personal safety. Be mindful of your surroundings, especially in crowded tourist areas

or unfamiliar neighborhoods, and avoid displaying valuables or carrying large amounts of cash. Use caution when using public transportation, and always keep your belongings secure. If you're exploring nightlife or entertainment districts, drink responsibly and make arrangements for safe transportation back to your accommodations. In case of emergencies or suspicious activity, don't hesitate to contact local law enforcement or seek assistance from trusted individuals or establishments.

Emergency Contacts:

In the event of an emergency or crisis situation in Colorado, knowing the appropriate contacts can make all the difference. For immediate assistance with police, fire, or medical emergencies, dial **911** from any phone. This universal emergency number connects you to the appropriate emergency services dispatcher who can dispatch assistance to your location. Additionally, it's a good idea to program local emergency contacts into your phone, including the non-emergency numbers for local law enforcement agencies, medical facilities, and search and rescue organizations. Having these numbers readily available can expedite the response time in case of emergencies and ensure that you receive the assistance you need promptly.

5.5 Currency, Banking, Budgeting and Money Matters

As you embark on your journey to Colorado, ensuring you have a solid understanding of currency, banking, and money matters is essential for a seamless travel experience. From exchanging currency to managing your budget, knowing the ins and outs of financial logistics can help you make the most of your time in the Centennial State without any monetary hiccups.

Currency Exchange:

The official currency of the United States is the US Dollar (USD), and it is widely accepted throughout Colorado. If you're arriving from a foreign country, you may need to exchange your home currency for USD upon arrival. While many major airports and tourist hubs offer currency exchange services, be mindful of potentially high fees and less favorable exchange rates. Consider exchanging a small amount of currency for immediate expenses and using ATMs or local banks for larger withdrawals once you've settled in.

Banking Services:

Colorado is home to a variety of banking institutions, ranging from large national banks to local credit unions and community banks. Most cities and towns in Colorado have multiple bank branches and ATMs, making it convenient to access banking services during your stay. Before traveling, notify your bank of your itinerary to prevent any potential issues with card usage or transactions flagged as suspicious due to out-of-state activity. Additionally, inquire about any international transaction fees or ATM withdrawal fees that may apply to your account to avoid unexpected charges.

ATM Access:

ATMs are widely available throughout Colorado, offering convenient access to cash withdrawals and banking services. Look for ATMs affiliated with major networks such as Visa, Mastercard, or American Express to ensure compatibility with your debit or credit cards. Keep in mind that some ATMs may charge fees for out-of-network withdrawals, so try to use ATMs affiliated with your bank or network whenever possible. It's also a good idea to withdraw large amounts of cash less frequently to minimize transaction fees and avoid running out of money unexpectedly.

Budgeting Tips:

Whether you're exploring Colorado's natural wonders, dining at local restaurants, or indulging in retail therapy, budgeting wisely can help you make the most of your travel funds. Start by creating a detailed budget that accounts for transportation, accommodations, meals, activities, and souvenirs. Research average costs for goods and services in the areas you plan to visit, and factor in any additional expenses such as admission fees, parking, or gratuities. Consider using cash for smaller purchases to better track your spending and avoid overspending on credit cards.

Credit Card Usage:

Credit cards are widely accepted throughout Colorado, especially in urban areas, hotels, restaurants, and larger retail establishments. Using a credit card can offer convenience, security, and certain protections for purchases. However, be mindful of potential foreign transaction fees, currency conversion fees, and interest rates that may apply to international transactions. Additionally, inform your credit card issuer of your travel plans to prevent any unexpected holds or declines due to suspected fraud.

5.6 Language, Communication and Useful Phrases

As you journey through the diverse landscapes and vibrant communities of Colorado, effective communication plays a vital role in enhancing your travel experience. While English is the predominant language spoken throughout the state, understanding regional dialects, cultural nuances, and useful phrases can help you navigate conversations with locals and immerse yourself in the rich tapestry of Colorado's cultural heritage.

English as the Primary Language:

English is the primary language spoken in Colorado, making it relatively easy for English-speaking visitors to communicate with locals. Whether you're ordering a meal at a restaurant, asking for directions, or striking up a conversation with a fellow traveler, English proficiency will serve you well in most situations. However, keep in mind that accents and colloquialisms may vary depending on the region, so don't be surprised if you encounter different linguistic quirks during your travels.

Regional Dialects and Expressions:

While standard American English is widely understood in Colorado, you may encounter regional dialects and expressions that reflect the state's diverse cultural heritage. In rural areas and smaller towns, you might hear distinctive accents or local phrases that add color to everyday conversations. Embracing these regional nuances can enrich your travel experience and foster connections with locals who appreciate your interest in their linguistic traditions.

Useful Phrases and Expressions:

While English proficiency is sufficient for most interactions in Colorado, learning a few useful phrases and expressions can enhance your communication skills and show respect for the local culture. Consider practicing common greetings such as "hello," "good morning," and "thank you," as well as polite phrases like "please" and "excuse me." Additionally, familiarize yourself with basic directions and transportation-related phrases to facilitate navigation around the state.

Cultural Etiquette:

In addition to language proficiency, understanding cultural etiquette and social norms can help you navigate interactions with locals in Colorado. Remember to greet people with a friendly smile and maintain a respectful demeanor in all interactions. When engaging in conversations, listen attentively and avoid interrupting others. If you're unsure about cultural customs or appropriate behavior in certain situations, don't hesitate to ask for guidance or clarification from locals or tour guides.

Embracing Diversity:

Colorado is home to a diverse population representing a wide range of cultural backgrounds and identities. Embracing this diversity fosters mutual respect and understanding among travelers and locals alike. Take the opportunity to learn about different cultural traditions, cuisines, and customs during your visit, and approach interactions with an open mind and a spirit of curiosity. By celebrating diversity and fostering cross-cultural connections, you'll enrich your travel experience and forge lasting memories in Colorado.

5.7 Useful Websites, Mobile Apps and Online Resources

In the digital age, travelers have access to a wealth of information and resources at their fingertips, making trip planning and navigation more convenient than ever. I've curated a selection of useful websites, mobile apps, and online resources to enhance your exploration of Colorado. From real-time weather updates to trail maps and cultural insights, these digital tools will enrich your travel experience in the Centennial State.

Weather and Road Conditions:

Before embarking on your Colorado adventure, it's essential to stay informed about current weather conditions and road conditions, especially if you'll be exploring mountainous terrain or remote areas. Websites such as the National Weather Service (https://www.weather.gov/) and the Colorado Department of Transportation (https://www.cotrip.org/) provide up-to-date forecasts, road closures, and traffic alerts to help you plan your itinerary and stay safe on the road.

Outdoor Recreation and Trails:

For outdoor enthusiasts seeking to explore Colorado's vast wilderness and scenic trails, mobile apps like AllTrails and Trailforks are invaluable resources. These apps offer detailed trail maps, user reviews, and real-time GPS navigation to help you discover hiking, biking, and off-road trails tailored to your preferences and skill level. Additionally, websites like https://www.colorado.com/ and https://www.visitcos.com/ provide comprehensive guides to outdoor recreation opportunities, including national parks, state parks, and recreational areas across the state.

Cultural Events and Attractions:

To immerse yourself in Colorado's rich cultural heritage and vibrant arts scene, websites such as https://www.denver.org/ and https://www.visitdenver.com/ offer calendars of events, museum listings, and insider tips on local attractions and landmarks. Whether you're interested in exploring Denver's bustling art districts, attending live music performances, or discovering hidden gems in small towns and communities, these online resources provide valuable insights to help you plan your cultural itinerary.

Dining and Culinary Experiences:

Colorado's culinary scene is as diverse as its landscapes, with a thriving food culture influenced by regional ingredients and culinary traditions. Websites like https://denver.eater.com/ and https://www.westword.com/ offer restaurant guides, reviews, and recommendations for dining establishments ranging from fine dining restaurants to casual eateries and food trucks. Additionally, mobile apps like Yelp (https://www.yelp.com/) and TripAdvisor (https://www.tripadvisor.com/ provide user-generated reviews and ratings to help you discover top-rated dining destinations and local favorites during your visit to Colorado.

Transportation and Transit:

Navigating Colorado's transportation network, including public transit options and ride-sharing services, is made easier with mobile apps like Uber, Lyft, and Transit *(Available on Google Play Store and Apple Play Store)*. These apps allow you to hail rides, plan routes, and track public transportation schedules in real-time, ensuring seamless navigation around cities and towns across the state. Additionally, websites like https://www.rtd-denver.com/ provide information on regional transit systems, including bus routes, light rail lines, and commuter rail services serving the Denver metropolitan area.

5.8 Visitor Centers and Tourist Assistance

For travelers exploring the diverse landscapes and attractions of Colorado, visitor centers and tourist assistance services serve as invaluable resources for information, guidance, and support. Here's a guide to visitor centers and tourist assistance in Colorado to enhance your travel experience in the Centennial State.

Colorado Tourism Office:

The Colorado Tourism Office (CTO) serves as the official state tourism agency, promoting Colorado as a premier travel destination and providing resources for visitors planning their trip. Located in Denver, the CTO offers a wealth of information on attractions, accommodations, events, and activities across the state. Their website, https://www.colorado.com/, features comprehensive guides, travel itineraries, and inspiration for exploring Colorado's diverse regions, making it a valuable online resource for travelers.

Local Visitor Centers:

Throughout Colorado, local visitor centers serve as hubs of information and assistance for travelers seeking guidance on nearby attractions, accommodations, dining options, and recreational activities. From mountain towns to urban centers, visitor centers are typically staffed with knowledgeable locals who can offer insider tips and recommendations for making the most of your visit. Websites like https://www.visitdenver.com/ and https://www.visitcos.com/ provide directories of visitor centers in major cities and tourist destinations across the state.

National Park Visitor Centers:

Colorado is home to several national parks and monuments, each with its own visitor center offering educational exhibits, interpretive programs, and resources for exploring the park. For example, Rocky Mountain National Park has visitor centers located at key entrances, including Beaver Meadows Visitor Center and Kawuneeche Visitor Center, where visitors can obtain maps, trail information, and updates on park conditions. The website of The National Park Service(https://www.nps.gov/) provides detailed information on visitor centers in Colorado's national parks, including operating hours and contact information.

Online Resources and Assistance:

In addition to in-person visitor centers, travelers can access a wealth of online resources and assistance to help plan their trip to Colorado. Websites like https://www.gocolorado.com/ and https://www.coloradoinfo.com/ offer directories of tourist information centers, visitor bureaus, and chambers of commerce across the state, providing contact information and links to additional resources. For real-time assistance, travelers can also reach out to Colorado's tourism hotline at **1-800-COLORADO** or utilize online chat services available on tourism websites.

Emergency Assistance and Support:

In the event of emergencies or unforeseen circumstances during your travels in Colorado, it's essential to know where to turn for assistance and support. In addition to contacting local law enforcement or emergency services by dialing **911**, travelers can seek assistance from their embassy or consulate if they are foreign nationals. Additionally, organizations like the American Red Cross and local community services may offer support for travelers in need of emergency assistance, shelter, or resources.

CHAPTER 6
CULINARY DELIGHTS

6.1 Restaurants and Cafes

Click the link or Scan QR Code with a device to view a comprehensive map of various Restaurants in Colorado – <u>*https://shorturl.at/oyL45*</u>

Colorado's culinary scene is as diverse as its landscapes, offering a tantalizing array of flavors and experiences for food enthusiasts. From cozy cafes serving artisanal coffee to upscale restaurants showcasing farm-to-table cuisine, the Centennial State has something to satisfy every palate. These restaurants and cafes in Colorado promise exceptional dining experiences for visitors seeking to indulge in the state's gastronomic delights.

The Buckhorn Exchange (Denver):
Located in Denver's historic Five Points neighborhood, The Buckhorn Exchange is a culinary institution renowned for its Old West charm and wild game cuisine. Established in 1893, it holds the title of Colorado's oldest restaurant and boasts a menu featuring exotic meats such as buffalo, elk, and rattlesnake. Diners can savor hearty dishes like Rocky Mountain oysters, bison steaks, and grilled quail in a rustic setting adorned with taxidermy trophies and memorabilia. The Buckhorn Exchange is open for dinner Tuesday through Saturday from 5:00 PM to 9:00 PM, making it an ideal destination for a memorable dining experience steeped in history.

Snooze, an A.M. Eatery (Colorado Springs):
For breakfast aficionados craving creative twists on classic morning fare, Snooze, an A.M. Eatery is a must-visit destination in Colorado Springs. With its retro-inspired decor and playful menu offerings, Snooze delights diners with dishes like pineapple upside-down pancakes, breakfast pot pie, and inventive Benedicts. The restaurant sources ingredients from local farms and purveyors whenever possible, ensuring fresh and flavorful dishes that showcase the best of Colorado's culinary bounty. Open daily from

6:30 AM to 2:30 PM, Snooze invites visitors to start their day with a delicious breakfast or brunch experience that's sure to leave a lasting impression.

The Kitchen (Boulder):

Nestled in the heart of downtown Boulder, The Kitchen is a farm-to-table restaurant dedicated to sustainable, seasonal cuisine and community engagement. Led by Executive Chef Hugo Matheson, The Kitchen celebrates Colorado's agricultural heritage with a menu highlighting locally sourced ingredients and artisanal products. Diners can enjoy dishes like roasted beet salad, Colorado lamb stew, and wood-fired pizzas in a warm and inviting atmosphere that reflects the restaurant's commitment to hospitality and shared dining experiences. The Kitchen is open for lunch Monday through Friday from 11:00 AM to 2:30 PM and for dinner Sunday through Thursday from 5:00 PM to 9:00 PM and Friday through Saturday from 5:00 PM to 10:00 PM.

Red Rocks Grill (Morrison):

Situated just minutes from the iconic Red Rocks Amphitheatre, Red Rocks Grill offers a dining experience that perfectly complements Colorado's outdoor lifestyle and natural beauty. With its scenic mountain views and casual yet refined ambiance, the restaurant specializes in contemporary American cuisine with a focus on locally sourced ingredients and bold flavors. Guests can enjoy dishes like Colorado bison burgers, grilled trout, and artisanal flatbreads while soaking in the panoramic vistas of the surrounding foothills. Red Rocks Grill is open for lunch and dinner daily, with hours varying depending on seasonal events and concert schedules at Red Rocks Amphitheatre.

The Little Bird Bakeshop (Fort Collins):

For those with a sweet tooth craving delectable pastries and artisanal baked goods, The Little Bird Bakeshop in Fort Collins is a hidden gem waiting to be discovered. This charming neighborhood bakery offers a tempting selection of cakes, cookies, croissants, and breads made from scratch using high-quality, locally sourced ingredients. From classic French macarons to savory scones and seasonal fruit tarts, every item at The Little Bird Bakeshop is crafted with care and attention to detail. The bakery is open Tuesday through Sunday from 7:00 AM to 3:00 PM, inviting visitors to indulge in a delightful pastry or treat while exploring the vibrant culinary scene of Fort Collins.

6.2 Bars and Pubs

Click the link or Scan QR Code with a device to view a comprehensive map of various Bars and Pubs in Colorado – https://shorturl.at/gjnzB

Colorado's nightlife is as diverse as its landscapes, with a plethora of bars and pubs offering unique atmospheres, craft beverages, and live entertainment. From historic saloons to trendy cocktail lounges, the Centennial State boasts an eclectic array of drinking establishments sure to satisfy every palate.

The Cruise Room (Denver):
Located in Denver's historic Oxford Hotel, The Cruise Room is a legendary Art Deco bar renowned for its vintage charm and classic cocktails. Opened in 1933, The Cruise Room is Denver's oldest bar and retains much of its original ambiance, with elegant decor inspired by the ocean liner era. Guests can enjoy signature drinks like the Moscow Mule or the Aviation while soaking in the bar's storied history and glamorous atmosphere. The Cruise Room is open daily from 4:00 PM to 12:00 AM, offering an ideal setting for pre-dinner drinks or late-night rendezvous.

The Barrel (Estes Park):
Nestled in the heart of downtown Estes Park, The Barrel is a unique taproom and beer garden offering a rotating selection of craft beers, ciders, and wines from local and regional breweries. What sets The Barrel apart is its self-serve tap system, allowing patrons to pour their own drinks and sample a variety of brews at their own pace. With a cozy indoor space and spacious outdoor patio, The Barrel is the perfect spot to unwind after a day of exploring Rocky Mountain National Park. Prices vary depending on the beverage selection, with options to purchase by the ounce or by the pint. The Barrel is open daily from 12:00 PM to 10:00

PM, inviting visitors to enjoy a laid-back drinking experience in the heart of Estes Park.

The Strater Hotel (Durango):
Steeped in history and Old West charm, The Strater Hotel in Durango is home to several iconic bars and lounges, each with its own distinct character and ambiance. The Diamond Belle Saloon, located within the hotel, transports guests back to the days of the Wild West with live ragtime piano music, swinging saloon doors, and period decor. Meanwhile, The Office Spiritorium offers a more refined setting for craft cocktails and small plates, featuring an extensive menu of classic and innovative libations. Prices at The Strater Hotel bars vary depending on the beverage selection and time of day, with happy hour specials and drink specials offered throughout the week. The Diamond Belle Saloon and The Office Spiritorium have different opening and closing hours, so visitors are advised to check the hotel's website for specific details.

The Bucksnort Saloon (Pine):
Tucked away in the mountain town of Pine, The Bucksnort Saloon is a rustic watering hole beloved by locals and visitors alike for its laid-back atmosphere and scenic mountain views. Housed in a historic log cabin dating back to the 1850s, The Bucksnort Saloon exudes frontier charm with its log beams, antler chandeliers, and wood-burning stove. The bar offers a selection of draft beers, cocktails, and pub grub, including burgers, sandwiches, and hearty appetizers. Prices at The Bucksnort Saloon are reasonable, with

options to suit every budget. The bar is open Wednesday through Sunday from 11:00 AM to 7:00 PM, providing a cozy retreat for patrons seeking a taste of Colorado's mountain hospitality.

The Bitter Bar (Boulder):

Nestled in downtown Boulder, The Bitter Bar is a hip cocktail lounge known for its innovative libations and chic ambiance. With a focus on craft cocktails made with premium spirits and house-made ingredients, The Bitter Bar offers a menu of creative concoctions sure to tantalize the taste buds. From classic cocktails like the Old Fashioned to modern creations like the Smoked Rosemary Paloma, there's something for every palate to enjoy. Prices at The Bitter Bar are in line with other upscale cocktail lounges, with happy hour specials available on select days. The bar is open daily from 4:00 PM to 11:00 PM, inviting guests to sip and savor in style against a backdrop of sleek decor and lively energy.

6.3 Local Food Markets and Festivals

Colorado's culinary landscape is rich and diverse, with an abundance of local food markets and festivals showcasing the state's agricultural bounty and vibrant food culture. From bustling farmers' markets to lively food festivals, these events offer visitors the opportunity to sample fresh produce, artisanal products, and culinary delights while immersing themselves in the spirit of community and celebration.

Union Station Farmers Market (Denver):

Located in the heart of downtown Denver at historic Union Station, the Union Station Farmers Market is a vibrant gathering place for local farmers, artisans, and food purveyors. Every Saturday from May to October, the market comes alive with stalls overflowing with fresh fruits, vegetables, meats, cheeses, baked goods, and more. Visitors can browse the diverse array of offerings, chat with vendors, and sample seasonal specialties while enjoying live music and entertainment. Prices vary depending on the products, but visitors can expect to find high-quality, locally sourced goods at reasonable prices. Tips for visitors include arriving early to beat the crowds, bringing reusable bags or baskets for shopping, and trying the gourmet food trucks parked nearby for a quick bite to eat.

Boulder Farmers Market (Boulder):

Nestled along Boulder Creek in downtown Boulder, the Boulder Farmers Market is a beloved community gathering place renowned for its commitment to local and sustainable agriculture. Open every Saturday and Wednesday from April to November, the market showcases an impressive selection of organic produce, artisanal cheeses, baked goods, flowers, and more. Visitors can peruse the stalls, chat with farmers and artisans, and enjoy live music and chef demonstrations. Prices at the Boulder Farmers Market vary depending on the season and the products, but visitors can expect to find high-quality, farm-fresh goods at competitive prices. Tips for visitors include bringing cash for transactions (although many vendors accept credit cards), wearing comfortable shoes for walking, and sampling the diverse array of ready-to-eat snacks and meals available at the market.

Telluride Bluegrass Festival (Telluride):

For music lovers and food enthusiasts alike, the Telluride Bluegrass Festival is a can't-miss event held annually in the picturesque mountain town of Telluride. In addition to world-class bluegrass performances on multiple stages, the festival features a delectable array of food vendors offering everything from gourmet grilled cheese sandwiches to artisanal ice cream and craft beverages. Visitors can enjoy meals alfresco while soaking in the stunning mountain views and festive atmosphere. Prices for food and beverages at the Telluride Bluegrass Festival vary depending on the vendor and the menu item, but visitors can expect to find a range of options to suit every taste and budget. Tips for visitors include purchasing festival tickets in advance, arriving early to secure a good spot, and exploring the nearby food and drink options in downtown Telluride between performances.

Colorado Springs Food Truck Fest (Colorado Springs):

For a taste of Colorado Springs' thriving food truck scene, visitors won't want to miss the Colorado Springs Food Truck Fest, held periodically throughout the year at various locations across the city. This family-friendly event brings together a diverse lineup of food trucks serving up everything from tacos and BBQ to gourmet grilled cheese and vegan fare. Visitors can stroll through the festival grounds, sampling a variety of culinary creations while enjoying live music, games, and entertainment. Prices for food truck fare at the festival vary depending on the vendor and the menu item, but visitors can expect to find affordable options for every palate. Tips for visitors include bringing cash for transactions (although some food trucks may accept credit cards), arriving early to avoid long lines, and trying a little bit of everything to experience the full range of flavors on offer.

Palisade Peach Festival (Palisade):

Located in the heart of Colorado's Western Slope, the Palisade Peach Festival is a celebration of the region's most famous fruit and the growers who cultivate it. Held annually in August, the festival offers visitors the chance to sample a wide variety of fresh peaches, peach-inspired dishes, and peach-infused beverages from local vendors. In addition to peach-centric fare, the festival features live music, arts and crafts vendors, cooking demonstrations, and family-friendly activities. Prices for peach products and festival food vary depending on the vendor and the menu item, but visitors can expect to find plenty of delicious options to satisfy their peach cravings. Tips for visitors include bringing sunscreen and hats for sun protection, arriving early to beat the crowds, and indulging in the festival's signature peach cobbler and ice cream for a sweet treat.

6.4 Culinary Tours and Classes

Colorado's culinary scene is a vibrant tapestry of flavors, influenced by the state's diverse cultural heritage and abundant natural resources. For visitors eager to immerse themselves in the culinary delights of the Centennial State, culinary tours and classes offer immersive experiences that showcase the best of Colorado's food and drink culture. From hands-on cooking classes to guided tours of local markets and farms, these culinary experiences provide a behind-the-scenes look at the ingredients, techniques, and traditions that shape Colorado's culinary landscape.

Local Table Tours (Boulder):

Located in the picturesque city of Boulder, Local Table Tours offers guided culinary walking tours that highlight the city's vibrant food scene and artisanal producers. Led by knowledgeable guides, participants embark on a leisurely stroll through downtown Boulder, stopping at local eateries, specialty food shops, and farmers' markets along the way. Guests have the opportunity to sample a variety of dishes, snacks, and beverages while learning about the history, culture, and sustainability practices of the businesses visited. Prices for Local Table Tours vary depending on the length and type of tour, with options to customize private tours for special occasions or group events. Tips for participants include wearing comfortable walking shoes, bringing a reusable water bottle, and arriving with an appetite for adventure and discovery.

The Seasoned Chef Cooking School (Denver):

For aspiring home chefs and culinary enthusiasts, The Seasoned Chef Cooking School in Denver offers a diverse range of hands-on cooking classes taught by professional chefs and culinary experts. From basic cooking techniques to advanced culinary skills, participants can choose from a variety of classes covering cuisines from around the world, as well as specialized workshops focusing on topics like baking, wine pairing, and knife skills. Classes are held in a state-of-the-art kitchen facility equipped with modern appliances and cooking stations, providing a supportive and interactive learning environment for students of all levels. Prices for classes at The Seasoned Chef Cooking School vary depending on the duration and complexity of the class, with discounts available for multi-class packages or group bookings. Tips for participants include arriving early to meet fellow classmates and instructors, wearing comfortable clothing and closed-toe shoes, and bringing a notebook to jot down recipes and cooking tips.

Colorado Cannabis Tours (Denver and Colorado Springs):

For those curious about Colorado's burgeoning cannabis industry and its culinary applications, Colorado Cannabis Tours offers immersive experiences that combine education, exploration, and tastings of cannabis-infused foods and beverages. Led by knowledgeable guides, participants visit dispensaries, grow facilities, and cannabis-infused product manufacturers to learn about the cultivation, extraction, and consumption of cannabis products in a legal and responsible manner. In addition to educational tours, Colorado Cannabis Tours also offers cooking classes and workshops where participants can learn how to prepare their own cannabis-infused dishes and beverages under the guidance of experienced chefs and cannabis experts. Prices for Colorado Cannabis Tours vary depending on the type and duration of the experience, with options to customize private tours for special occasions or group events. Tips for participants include consuming cannabis responsibly and in accordance with state laws, being mindful of personal tolerance levels, and staying hydrated throughout the tour or class.

Rocky Mountain Food Tours (Colorado Springs):
Based in Colorado Springs, Rocky Mountain Food Tours offers guided walking tours that showcase the city's culinary diversity and local flavors. Led by passionate foodies and knowledgeable guides, participants embark on a leisurely stroll through historic downtown Colorado Springs, stopping at a variety of restaurants, cafes, and specialty food shops to sample a range of dishes and culinary creations. Along the way, guests learn about the city's history, architecture, and culinary traditions while enjoying behind-the-scenes access to some of the area's top dining destinations. Prices for Rocky Mountain Food Tours vary depending on the length and type of tour, with options to customize private tours for special occasions or group events. Tips for participants include wearing comfortable walking shoes, bringing a reusable water bottle, and arriving with an open mind

and adventurous palate ready to discover new flavors and culinary delights.

Cheese Making Classes at Haystack Mountain Creamery (Longmont):

For cheese lovers and dairy enthusiasts, Haystack Mountain Creamery in Longmont offers hands-on cheese making classes that provide a unique opportunity to learn the art and science of crafting artisanal cheeses. Led by experienced cheese makers, participants learn about the cheese making process from start to finish, including milk selection, curd formation, pressing, aging, and flavor development. Classes are held in the creamery's production facility, where participants have the chance to work with high-quality milk and equipment while receiving personalized instruction and guidance. Prices for cheese making classes at Haystack Mountain Creamery vary depending on the duration and type of class, with options to take home freshly made cheeses and cheese making kits. Tips for participants include wearing comfortable clothing and closed-toe shoes, bringing a sense of curiosity and enthusiasm for learning, and preparing to get hands-on with the cheese making process from start to finish.

6.5 Dietary Restrictions and Specialties

Colorado's culinary scene is as diverse as its landscapes, offering a wide array of dining options to suit every palate and dietary preference. Whether you're a vegetarian, vegan, gluten-free, or have other dietary restrictions, you'll find that the Centennial State is home to a plethora of restaurants, cafes, and specialty shops that cater to various dietary needs. As an author of travel guides and a culinary enthusiast, I've explored Colorado's dining scene and compiled insights into navigating dietary restrictions and specialties in the state.

Vegetarian and Vegan Options:

For vegetarians and vegans, Colorado offers a wealth of dining options showcasing plant-based cuisine at its finest. From trendy vegan cafes to upscale vegetarian restaurants, visitors will find no shortage of delicious meat-free dishes to enjoy. Denver, Boulder, and Colorado Springs are particularly known for their vibrant vegetarian and vegan scenes, with establishments like WaterCourse Foods in Denver, Leaf Vegetarian Restaurant in Boulder, and Adam's Mountain Cafe in Colorado Springs leading the charge in offering creative and flavorful plant-based fare. These restaurants often feature seasonal and locally sourced ingredients, ensuring fresh and wholesome meals that satisfy even the most discerning palate.

Gluten-Free Dining:

Navigating gluten-free dining options in Colorado is made easier by the state's growing awareness of gluten intolerance and celiac disease. Many restaurants now offer gluten-free menus or indicate gluten-free options on their regular menus, making it easier for diners with gluten sensitivities to find suitable dishes. In cities like Denver and Boulder, dedicated gluten-free bakeries and cafes, such as Deby's Gluten-Free Bakery in Denver and Shine Restaurant & Potion Bar in Boulder, offer a wide selection of gluten-free baked goods, pastries, and entrees. Additionally, ethnic cuisines like Mexican, Thai, and Japanese often feature naturally gluten-free dishes, providing additional options for gluten-conscious diners.

Farm-to-Table and Locally Sourced Fare:
For visitors seeking a taste of Colorado's agricultural bounty, farm-to-table restaurants and eateries specializing in locally sourced cuisine are the way to go. These establishments prioritize fresh, seasonal ingredients sourced from local farms, ranches, and producers, resulting in dishes that are not only delicious but also environmentally sustainable. Restaurants like Black Cat Bistro in Boulder, The Kitchen in Denver, and Four by Brother Luck in Colorado Springs are renowned for their commitment to sourcing ingredients locally and supporting Colorado's farmers and artisans. Visitors can expect menus that change with the seasons, reflecting the best of Colorado's agricultural offerings at any given time.

Craft Breweries and Gluten-Free Beer:
Colorado's craft beer scene is world-renowned, but what about those with gluten sensitivities or celiac disease? Fortunately, several breweries in Colorado offer gluten-free beer options, ensuring that everyone can partake in the state's craft beer culture. Breweries like Holidaily Brewing Company in Golden specialize exclusively in gluten-free beers, offering a variety of

styles crafted from gluten-free grains like millet and sorghum. Additionally, many traditional craft breweries now offer gluten-reduced or gluten-removed beers, providing options for those with milder gluten sensitivities to enjoy a pint without worry.

Ethnic Cuisine and International Flavors:

Exploring Colorado's diverse culinary landscape wouldn't be complete without sampling the state's wide array of ethnic cuisines and international flavors. Whether you're craving spicy Indian curries, flavorful Ethiopian stews, or traditional Japanese sushi, you'll find a melting pot of international cuisines represented in Colorado's dining scene. Cities like Denver, Aurora, and Boulder boast vibrant ethnic neighborhoods where visitors can embark on culinary adventures through Little Ethiopia, Havana Street, or Federal Boulevard, discovering hidden gems and authentic flavors from around the globe. Many of these establishments offer vegetarian, vegan, and gluten-free options, making it easier for diners with dietary restrictions to indulge in a world of culinary delights.

CHAPTER 7

CULTURE AND HERITAGE

7.1 Museums and Galleries

Colorado, with its breathtaking landscapes and vibrant culture, is home to a myriad of museums and galleries that offer visitors a window into its diverse history and artistic legacy. From ancient artifacts to contemporary masterpieces, each institution holds treasures waiting to be discovered.

Denver Art Museum

Located in the heart of Denver, the Denver Art Museum stands as a beacon of artistic expression in the Rocky Mountain region. Situated at 100 W 14th Ave Pkwy, Denver, CO 80204, this cultural landmark welcomes visitors with its striking architecture and extensive collection spanning centuries and continents. The museum is open from 10:00 AM to 5:00 PM on weekdays and Saturdays, with extended hours until 8:00 PM on Fridays. On Sundays, operating hours are from 10:00 AM to 5:00 PM. To immerse oneself in the world of art at the Denver Art Museum, visitors can purchase tickets either online or at the museum's entrance. The entry fee for adults is $25, while seniors (65+) and military personnel enjoy a discounted rate of $20. College students with valid ID can enter for $18, and youth (ages 6–18) for $5 while children under the age of 5 have free entry. Additionally, the museum offers membership programs for those eager to delve deeper into its exhibitions and programs. The Denver Art Museum boasts a diverse collection encompassing American Indian, European, Asian, African, and American art, among others. From ancient artifacts to contemporary installations, each gallery offers a unique journey through human creativity and expression. Visitors can also participate in guided tours, educational programs, and special events hosted by the museum throughout the year, enriching their cultural experience.

Museum of Contemporary Art Denver
Nestled in the vibrant neighborhood of LoDo (Lower Downtown), the Museum of Contemporary Art Denver (MCA Denver) embodies the avant-garde spirit of modern art. Located at 1485 Delgany St, Denver, CO 80202, this dynamic institution showcases cutting-edge works by both established and emerging artists,

pushing the boundaries of artistic innovation. Operating hours at MCA Denver are from 10:00 AM to 6:00 PM from Tuesday to Sunday, with extended hours until 9:00 PM on Fridays. The museum is closed on Mondays. Admission to MCA Denver grants visitors access to its thought-provoking exhibitions, engaging programming, and captivating events. General admission tickets are priced at $10 for adults, $5 for seniors (65+), military personnel, and students with valid ID, and free for children under the age of 18. The museum also offers free admission to all on the first Saturday of every month, fostering accessibility and inclusivity within the community. At MCA Denver, visitors can explore a diverse array of contemporary artworks spanning various mediums, from painting and sculpture to video installations and performance art. The museum's commitment to fostering dialogue and experimentation makes it a hub for cultural exchange and artistic exploration. Additionally, MCA Denver hosts artist talks, workshops, and film screenings, providing visitors with immersive experiences that resonate long after their visit.

History Colorado Center

For those eager to delve into Colorado's rich history and heritage, the History Colorado Center offers a captivating journey through time. Located at 1200 Broadway, Denver, CO 80203, this state-of-the-art museum chronicles the story of Colorado, from its indigenous roots to its modern-day innovations. The History Colorado Center welcomes visitors from 10:00 AM to 5:00 PM from Monday to Saturday, and from 12:00 PM to 5:00 PM on

Sundays. Admission to the History Colorado Center grants access to its immersive exhibitions, interactive displays, and engaging programs designed to illuminate the past and inspire future generations. The entry fee for adults is $14, while seniors (65+), students (ages 13–22), and military personnel can enter for $12. Youth (ages 6–12) receive a discounted rate of $10, while children under the age of 5 enjoy free admission. Additionally, the museum offers membership options for those seeking to delve deeper into Colorado's history and culture. Visitors to the History Colorado Center can explore a diverse range of exhibits, including artifacts from the state's mining era, interactive displays highlighting the struggles and triumphs of Colorado's diverse communities, and immersive experiences that bring history to life. From the ancient Ancestral Puebloans to the pioneers of the Old West, each gallery offers a glimpse into the people and events that have shaped Colorado's identity.

Colorado Springs Fine Arts Center at Colorado College
Nestled in the scenic city of Colorado Springs, the Colorado Springs Fine Arts Center at Colorado College (FAC) blends art, education, and community to enrich the cultural landscape of the region. Located at 30 W Dale St, Colorado Springs, CO 80903, this multidisciplinary institution offers a diverse array of artistic experiences for visitors of all ages. The Colorado Springs Fine Arts Center welcomes visitors from 10:00 AM to 5:00 PM from Tuesday to Saturday, and from 1:00 PM to 5:00 PM on Sundays. The museum remains closed on Mondays. Admission to the FAC

grants visitors access to its extensive collection of American art, as well as rotating exhibitions showcasing works from around the world. The entry fee for adults is $20, while seniors (65+), military personnel, and students with valid ID can enter for $18. Youth (ages 6–18) receive a discounted rate of $10, while children under the age of 6 enjoy free admission. The museum also offers membership programs for those seeking to deepen their engagement with the arts. Visitors to the FAC can explore a wide range of artistic mediums, from painting and sculpture to photography and performance art. The museum's commitment to education is reflected in its diverse array of programs, including art classes, workshops, and lectures designed to inspire creativity and foster a deeper appreciation for the arts. Additionally, the FAC hosts community events, film screenings, and live performances, making it a vibrant cultural hub in the heart of Colorado Springs.

Boulder Museum of Contemporary Art

Tucked away in the eclectic city of Boulder, the Boulder Museum of Contemporary Art (BMoCA) celebrates the innovative spirit of contemporary art through thought-provoking exhibitions and dynamic programming. Located at 1750 13th St, Boulder, CO 80302, this intimate museum offers an intimate setting for artistic exploration and discovery. BMoCA is open to visitors from 11:00 AM to 6:00 PM from Tuesday to Sunday, and remains closed on Mondays. Admission to BMoCA grants visitors access to its rotating exhibitions featuring works by local, national, and international artists. The entry fee for adults is $5, while seniors

(65+), students with valid ID, and educators can enter for $4. Youth (ages 13–18) receive a discounted rate of $3, while children under the age of 12 enjoy free admission. The museum also offers free admission to all on the first Friday of every month, as part of Boulder's Art Night Out event. At BMoCA, visitors can immerse themselves in a diverse range of contemporary artworks, from abstract paintings and avant-garde sculptures to experimental installations and multimedia experiences. The museum's commitment to fostering creativity and dialogue is evident in its educational programs, artist residencies, and community partnerships. Visitors can also participate in gallery talks, workshops, and special events that offer unique insights into the creative process and the role of art in society.

7.2 Performing Arts and Theater

Colorado's diverse cultural landscape is not only enriched by its museums and galleries but also by its thriving performing arts and theater scene. From classic plays to cutting-edge performances, each theater offers visitors a unique opportunity to experience the magic of live entertainment.

Denver Center for the Performing Arts

Nestled in the heart of downtown Denver, the Denver Center for the Performing Arts (DCPA) stands as a cultural hub for theater enthusiasts and performing arts aficionados alike. Located at 1101 13th St, Denver, CO 80204, this iconic institution encompasses multiple theaters, each showcasing a diverse array of productions ranging from Broadway musicals to contemporary dramas. The Denver Center for the Performing Arts operates on varying schedules depending on the performance calendar. Generally, performances are held in the evenings on weekdays, with matinee shows available on weekends. Ticket prices vary depending on the production and seating arrangement, with discounts available for students, seniors, and members. It's advisable to check the DCPA website or box office for specific showtimes, ticket availability, and pricing. Visitors to the DCPA can expect a world-class theater experience, complete with state-of-the-art facilities, top-tier talent, and captivating productions that span genres and styles. From beloved classics to bold new works, each performance at the DCPA promises to enchant, inspire, and leave a lasting impression on audiences of all ages.

Boulder Theater
Situated in the vibrant city of Boulder, the Boulder Theater stands as a beacon of entertainment, hosting a wide range of live performances, concerts, and events throughout the year. Located at 2032 14th St, Boulder, CO 80302, this historic venue exudes charm and character, drawing visitors from near and far with its eclectic programming and intimate atmosphere. The Boulder Theater's schedule varies depending on the events and performances scheduled. Showtimes can range from early evening to late-night, with doors typically opening one hour before the start of the show. Ticket prices also vary depending on the event, with discounts available for students and members. It's

recommended to check the Boulder Theater website or box office for up-to-date information on showtimes, ticket availability, and pricing. Visitors to the Boulder Theater can immerse themselves in a wide range of entertainment options, including live music concerts, stand-up comedy shows, film screenings, and theatrical performances. With its historic charm and diverse lineup of events, the Boulder Theater offers something for everyone, ensuring an unforgettable experience for patrons of all tastes and interests.

Red Rocks Amphitheatre

Perched amidst the breathtaking natural beauty of Red Rocks Park and Amphitheatre, this iconic outdoor venue offers a truly unforgettable setting for live performances and concerts. Located at 18300 W Alameda Pkwy, Morrison, CO 80465, Red Rocks Amphitheatre has become synonymous with world-class entertainment and unparalleled acoustics, attracting top artists and performers from around the globe. Showtimes at Red Rocks Amphitheatre vary depending on the scheduled events and performances, with concerts and shows typically held in the evenings. Gates usually open several hours before the start of the show, allowing patrons to explore the stunning surroundings and enjoy pre-show festivities. Ticket prices vary depending on the artist and seating options, with general admission and reserved seating available for most events. Visitors to Red Rocks Amphitheatre can expect an immersive concert experience unlike any other, surrounded by towering red rock formations and panoramic views of the Colorado landscape. Whether attending a rock concert, electronic dance music festival, or yoga session at sunrise, patrons are sure to be mesmerized by the natural beauty and awe-inspiring ambiance of this legendary venue.

Arvada Center for the Arts and Humanities

Located in the charming suburb of Arvada, the Arvada Center for the Arts and Humanities serves as a cultural oasis, offering a diverse array of performing arts productions, visual arts exhibitions, and educational programs for audiences of all ages. Situated at 6901 Wadsworth Blvd, Arvada, CO 80003, this dynamic institution is committed to enriching the community through creativity, collaboration, and artistic excellence. The Arvada Center's performance schedule varies depending on the season, with theater productions typically held in the evenings and matinee shows available on weekends. Ticket prices vary depending on the production and seating options, with discounts available for students, seniors, and members. It's recommended to check the Arvada Center website or box office for specific showtimes, ticket availability, and pricing. Visitors to the Arvada Center can enjoy a wide range of theatrical experiences, including classic plays, contemporary dramas, musicals, and more. With its state-of-the-art theaters, talented performers, and engaging productions, the Arvada Center offers a vibrant cultural experience that inspires, entertains, and fosters a deeper appreciation for the arts.

Theatre Aspen

Nestled in the picturesque town of Aspen, Theatre Aspen showcases the best of live theater against the backdrop of the majestic Rocky Mountains. Located at 110 E Hallam St, Aspen, CO 81611, this renowned theater company produces a diverse array of productions ranging from Broadway musicals to intimate dramas, attracting audiences from across the country to its scenic outdoor venue and intimate indoor theater. The performance schedule at Theatre Aspen varies depending on the season, with productions typically held in the evenings and matinee performances available on select dates. Ticket prices vary depending on the production and seating options, with discounts available for students, seniors, and members. It's advisable to check the Theatre Aspen website or box office for specific showtimes, ticket availability, and pricing. Visitors to Theatre Aspen can expect a world-class theater experience amidst the stunning natural beauty of Aspen, with top-notch performances, innovative productions, and unparalleled hospitality.

7.3 Indigenous Culture and Traditions

Colorado's indigenous tradition and culture offer a unique and vibrant window into the state's rich history. The indigenous peoples of Colorado, including the Ute, Arapaho, and Cheyenne tribes, have a long-standing history with the land that stretches back thousands of years. Their customs, practices, and stories are deeply intertwined with the natural landscape and hold a sacred reverence for the land. For intending visitors, exploring these traditions provides an opportunity to connect with the profound cultural heritage of the region.

Historical Background

The indigenous tribes of Colorado have lived in the region for millennia, long before European settlers arrived. The Ute people are among the oldest residents of the state, with their history rooted in the mountainous regions of Colorado. The Arapaho and Cheyenne tribes also inhabited the plains of eastern Colorado. These tribes each have their own distinct cultural practices, beliefs, and languages, which have been passed down through generations.

Spiritual Connection to the Land

For the indigenous peoples of Colorado, the land is more than just a physical space—it is a source of spiritual power and identity. Mountains, rivers, and other natural features are revered as sacred and are often associated with creation stories and ancestral spirits. These spiritual connections are reflected in ceremonies, rituals, and artistic expressions, providing visitors with a deep sense of reverence and respect for the environment.

Traditional Art and Crafts

Indigenous art and crafts play an essential role in preserving and celebrating the culture of Colorado's tribes. Traditional beadwork, pottery, basketry, and textiles showcase intricate designs and vibrant colors that are symbolic of the natural world and tribal history. Visitors can find these artistic expressions at cultural centers, museums, and events, offering a glimpse into the craftsmanship and creativity of the indigenous peoples.

Music and Dance

Music and dance are central to indigenous tradition, serving as a means of storytelling, celebration, and connection. The rhythmic beats of drums and the sounds of traditional flutes accompany ceremonial dances that tell stories of creation, migration, and life on the land. Visitors may have the opportunity to witness these performances at powwows and other cultural gatherings, where the beauty and energy of indigenous music and dance come alive.

Language and Oral Tradition

Language is a key component of indigenous culture, serving as a bridge to the past and a means of preserving tribal identity. The Ute, Arapaho, and Cheyenne languages each have their own unique structures and sounds. Oral tradition plays a vital role in passing down history, values, and teachings from one generation to the next. Listening to tribal elders share stories and wisdom provides an intimate connection to the rich cultural tapestry of the region.

Preserving Indigenous Heritage

Efforts to preserve and celebrate indigenous heritage are ongoing in Colorado. Cultural centers, such as the Ute Indian Museum in Montrose and the Southern Ute Cultural Center and Museum in

Ignacio, provide spaces for education and reflection on indigenous history and culture. These centers offer exhibits, workshops, and events that showcase the contributions and resilience of Colorado's tribes.

Modern Indigenous Life

Today, indigenous communities in Colorado continue to navigate the complexities of modern life while honoring their traditions. Many tribes are actively engaged in initiatives to preserve their cultural heritage, protect their lands, and support their communities. Visitors can support these efforts by attending cultural events, purchasing indigenous-made crafts, and respecting tribal lands and customs.

7.4 Historic Sites and Monuments

When you visit Colorado, you'll encounter a state rich in history and culture. The land, once home to Native American tribes such as the Ute and Arapaho, became a destination for explorers, settlers, miners, and visionaries in search of a new life in the American West. As you journey through Colorado, you'll find yourself surrounded by breathtaking landscapes, from the rugged Rocky Mountains to the expansive plains, as well as numerous historical landmarks and monuments. These sites not only serve as reminders of the state's storied past but also offer insight into the people and events that have shaped its identity. Here are some must-visit historical landmarks and monuments in Colorado.

Mesa Verde National Park

Mesa Verde National Park is a true gem of Colorado's archaeological heritage. The park is home to some of the best-preserved ancient cliff dwellings in North America, providing a glimpse into the lives of the Ancestral Puebloans who lived there over 700 years ago. As you explore the park, you'll be captivated by the cliff dwellings that seem to blend seamlessly into the rock formations. Cliff Palace, the largest and most iconic of the dwellings, is a must-see, with its intricate stone structures and kivas that tell the story of a sophisticated society. Tours led by rangers offer in-depth information about the history and culture of the Puebloans, making the visit both educational and awe-inspiring.

Bent's Old Fort

Bent's Old Fort National Historic Site is a living history experience that transports visitors back to the 19th century. This reconstructed adobe trading post was once a bustling center of trade between trappers, traders, Native American tribes, and settlers on the Santa Fe Trail. As you walk through the fort, you'll encounter interpreters dressed in period attire who bring the past to life by demonstrating crafts and daily activities of the time. The fort's strategic location along the Arkansas River made it an important hub for the exchange of goods and ideas. Visiting Bent's Old Fort provides a vivid understanding of the complexities and challenges of life on the frontier.

Molly Brown House Museum

In the heart of Denver, the Molly Brown House Museum stands as a testament to the life of one of the city's most notable residents, Margaret "Molly" Brown. Known for surviving the Titanic disaster and her philanthropic work, Brown's life was one of resilience and determination. The museum, housed in her beautifully restored Victorian-era home, offers guided tours that showcase her legacy and the impact she had on her community. Visitors can admire the elegant architecture, period furnishings, and Brown's personal belongings while learning about her involvement in social issues, including women's suffrage and workers' rights.

Red Rocks Amphitheatre

Red Rocks Amphitheatre is more than just a world-renowned music venue—it's a natural wonder and a historic landmark. Carved into the stunning red sandstone formations, the amphitheatre has been hosting events since the early 1900s. The acoustics of the venue are unmatched, providing concertgoers with an unforgettable experience as they enjoy performances under the open sky. During the day, visitors can hike the trails around the amphitheatre and take in the breathtaking views of the surrounding area. The visitor center features exhibits about the history and geology of the site, offering a deeper understanding of its significance.

Pikes Peak Cog Railway

The Pikes Peak Cog Railway is an iconic way to experience the majesty of Pikes Peak, one of Colorado's most famous mountains. The railway has been transporting visitors to the summit since the late 19th century, providing a unique and scenic journey through a variety of ecosystems. As you ascend the mountain, you'll witness the landscape transform from lush forests to alpine tundra, with sweeping views of the plains below. At the summit, you can explore the new summit complex, which includes a visitor center, café, and interactive exhibits about the mountain's history and geology. The journey on the Pikes Peak Cog Railway is a must-do for any visitor to Colorado, offering a memorable and breathtaking experience.

7.5 Artisan Communities and Workshops

When it comes to artisanal craftsmanship and unique community shopping experiences, Colorado offers a vibrant and diverse array of options. The state is home to talented artisans who create a wide range of goods, from handmade jewelry and pottery to carefully crafted leather goods and fine woodwork. These artisanal workshops and communities are often nestled in charming towns or bustling urban centers, providing visitors with a chance to explore the local culture and take home a special piece of Colorado. .

Salida's Creative District

Located in the heart of the Arkansas River Valley, Salida is a town that thrives on its artistic spirit. Its Creative District is a hub for artisans and makers, with a focus on fostering a vibrant community of creative talent. The district is home to a variety of workshops and studios where visitors can find handcrafted goods such as jewelry, pottery, and textiles. A stroll through downtown Salida reveals charming galleries, boutique shops, and a welcoming atmosphere that invites you to engage with local artists and their work. Salida's Creative District is easily accessible by car from major cities like Denver or Colorado Springs, making it a convenient destination for a day trip or weekend getaway.

Manitou Springs' Historic District

Nestled at the foot of Pikes Peak, Manitou Springs is a picturesque town known for its artistic community and natural beauty. The historic district features a mix of galleries and artisanal shops offering unique handcrafted items such as leather goods, ceramics, and paintings. The town's quaint streets are lined with colorful buildings and dotted with outdoor sculptures, creating an inviting environment for a leisurely shopping experience. Manitou Springs can be reached by car from Colorado Springs in just a short drive, making it a popular destination for both locals and tourists seeking an artistic escape.

RiNo Art District in Denver

Denver's RiNo (River North) Art District is a vibrant and ever-evolving neighborhood that has become a hub for contemporary art and creative businesses. The district is home to numerous galleries, studios, and artisanal shops where visitors can discover innovative works in various mediums, including glassblowing, metalwork, and urban art. RiNo's distinctive street art adds a splash of color and character to the area, while its proximity to downtown Denver makes it easily accessible for visitors exploring the city. The district's lively atmosphere and diverse selection of artistic goods make it a must-visit destination for anyone interested in supporting local creators.

Paonia's Creative Community

Nestled in the North Fork Valley, Paonia is a small town with a strong sense of community and a commitment to supporting local artisans. The town's creative community includes a variety of workshops and studios where visitors can find handmade goods such as fine woodwork, jewelry, and textiles. Paonia's natural surroundings and agricultural heritage also inspire the production of artisanal foods and beverages, including locally made wines and ciders. The town is about a three-hour drive from Denver, making it a peaceful retreat for those seeking a more intimate and rural artistic experience.

Boulder's Pearl Street Mall

Boulder's Pearl Street Mall is a pedestrian-friendly outdoor shopping district that showcases the city's eclectic and artistic spirit. The mall is home to a variety of boutiques and artisanal shops where visitors can find carefully crafted goods such as handcrafted soaps, candles, and unique fashion items. In addition to shopping, the mall offers a lively atmosphere with street performers, art installations, and local eateries. Pearl Street Mall is easily accessible from Denver by car or public transportation, making it a convenient and enjoyable destination for a day of shopping and exploration.

CHAPTER 8
OUTDOOR ACTIVITIES AND ADVENTURES

8.1 Hiking and Trekking

Hiking and trekking in Colorado offer an unparalleled outdoor adventure that invites visitors to immerse themselves in the state's breathtaking natural beauty. Known for its majestic Rocky Mountains, Colorado boasts an array of diverse landscapes, from alpine meadows and dense forests to sweeping plains and dramatic canyons. Whether you're an experienced mountaineer or a casual hiker, Colorado offers a variety of trails and trekking opportunities that cater to all skill levels. With stunning vistas around every bend and the chance to encounter abundant wildlife, a hike in Colorado is a truly transformative experience.

Exploring the Rocky Mountains

The Rocky Mountains form the spine of Colorado, running from north to south and encompassing numerous peaks, including some of the highest in the United States. Hiking in the Rockies is a must-do for any visitor to Colorado. Trails wind through lush valleys, alongside rushing streams, and up steep inclines to reach stunning summits. Imagine trekking through the fresh scent of pine trees, with the sound of a distant waterfall creating a symphony of nature. As you ascend, the air becomes crisp, and panoramic views unfold, revealing the expanse of the mountain range. One of the most popular destinations for hikers is Rocky Mountain National Park, which features over 350 miles of trails that take you through diverse ecosystems. From the iconic Bear Lake Loop, perfect for families and beginners, to the challenging Longs Peak trail for experienced climbers, the park offers something for everyone. Along the way, you may spot elk grazing in the meadows or catch a glimpse of a soaring eagle above.

Exploring High Alpine Lakes

Colorado's high alpine lakes offer a serene and captivating hiking experience. Nestled in the mountains, these crystal-clear lakes provide a perfect destination for a day hike or an overnight adventure. Imagine hiking to Emerald Lake in Rocky Mountain National Park, where the lake's glassy surface reflects the surrounding peaks. Or picture trekking to Crater Lake in the Maroon Bells-Snowmass Wilderness, where the iconic Maroon Bells provide a stunning backdrop for your journey. The trek to these lakes often involves a moderate climb through forests and meadows, but the reward at the end is always worth the effort. You might even find yourself having a peaceful picnic by the water's edge or taking a refreshing dip in the cool mountain waters.

Journeying Through Aspen Groves

Colorado is known for its vibrant autumn foliage, particularly the golden aspen groves that light up the mountainsides in late September and early October. Hiking through these groves is a magical experience, as the leaves shimmer in the sunlight and create a golden canopy above. One popular trail for experiencing the aspen groves is the Maroon Bells Scenic Loop near Aspen, where you can walk through dense stands of aspens while surrounded by the rugged peaks of the Elk Mountains. The sounds of leaves rustling in the breeze and the crunch of fallen leaves underfoot add to the sensory experience of hiking through these areas. Whether you're a seasoned hiker or just starting out, the beauty of Colorado's aspen groves is sure to leave a lasting impression.

Discovering Unique Geological Features

Colorado's geological diversity provides hikers with opportunities to explore unique and striking landscapes. The red rock formations of the Garden of the Gods in Colorado Springs are a prime example. Here, you can hike through towering sandstone spires and dramatic rock formations that have been shaped by time and weather. The trails are accessible and offer stunning views of the surrounding area, including the distant Pikes Peak. Another extraordinary destination is the Flatirons in Boulder, where distinctive flat-topped rock formations rise dramatically from the foothills. The Flatirons offer a variety of trails for hikers, from easy walks along the base to more challenging climbs up the rock faces.

Preparing for Your Adventure

When planning your hiking or trekking adventure in Colorado, it's important to be well-prepared. The weather can change rapidly in the mountains, so dressing in layers is key. Sturdy hiking boots, a hat, and sunscreen are also essential. Bring plenty of water and snacks to keep your energy up during the hike, and always follow Leave No Trace principles to help preserve the natural beauty of the area. Visitors new to the region, guided hikes are a great way to explore with an expert who can provide insights into the local flora, fauna, and history. Additionally, many parks and wilderness areas offer trail maps and information at visitor centers to help you plan your trip.

8.2 Skiing and Snowboarding

Skiing and snowboarding in Colorado provide a thrilling outdoor adventure that is second to none. As a winter wonderland with legendary snow-covered peaks, Colorado is a premier destination for winter sports enthusiasts from around the world. From world-class ski resorts and pristine mountain landscapes to cozy après-ski experiences and charming mountain towns, Colorado has something for everyone, whether you're a seasoned pro or a first-time skier or snowboarder.

World-Class Ski Resorts

Colorado is home to a wide variety of world-renowned ski resorts, each offering its own unique blend of terrain, amenities, and atmosphere. Places like Vail, Aspen Snowmass, and Breckenridge have become iconic in the world of winter sports, attracting skiers and snowboarders of all skill levels. These resorts boast a wealth of features such as meticulously groomed trails, challenging black diamond runs, extensive lift systems, and a variety of terrain parks for freestyle enthusiasts. Vail, for instance, is known for its vast skiable area and seven distinct back bowls, offering an expansive playground for adventure seekers. Aspen Snowmass features four interconnected mountains, providing diverse terrain for different skill levels and preferences. Breckenridge combines a historic mining town charm with a lively ski culture, making it a favorite among visitors.

Spectacular Snow Conditions

One of the reasons Colorado is such a top destination for skiing and snowboarding is its exceptional snow conditions. The state's high elevation and dry climate create perfect powdery snow that makes for smooth, exhilarating runs down the mountain. Whether you're carving down a groomed slope or navigating through the trees in search of untouched powder, the snow in Colorado provides an unmatched skiing and snowboarding experience. The season typically begins in November and can last well into April, depending on the resort's location and elevation. This extended season allows visitors ample time to experience the magic of skiing and snowboarding in Colorado.

Beginner-Friendly Options

If you're new to skiing or snowboarding, Colorado's resorts offer a variety of beginner-friendly options to help you get started. Many resorts have dedicated learning areas with gentle slopes, making it easy and safe to practice your turns. Professional instructors are available for lessons, providing valuable guidance and tips to help you build confidence on the snow. Once you've mastered the basics, you can gradually explore more challenging terrain and expand your skills. Resorts often offer progression parks, where you can practice tricks and techniques in a controlled environment.

Backcountry Adventures

For those seeking a more adventurous and off-the-beaten-path experience, Colorado's backcountry offers opportunities for ski touring and splitboarding. The vast wilderness areas and national forests provide access to untouched powder and breathtaking alpine landscapes. Exploring the backcountry requires proper preparation, including avalanche safety gear and knowledge, as conditions can be unpredictable. Guided backcountry tours are available for those who want to experience the beauty of the mountains while staying safe. Expert guides can lead you through pristine terrain and share their knowledge of the area, providing a truly unforgettable adventure.

Après-Ski Culture

After a day on the slopes, Colorado's après-ski culture offers a warm and welcoming atmosphere to unwind and relax. Cozy mountain lodges, lively bars, and charming restaurants provide the perfect setting to share stories of the day's adventures with friends and family. Many resorts offer a range of dining options, from casual fare to gourmet meals, as well as hot tubs and spa facilities for a soothing soak or massage. In addition to traditional après-ski spots, many mountain towns host a variety of events and festivals throughout the winter season, celebrating the joy of the season with live music, local craft beverages, and unique culinary experiences.

Preparing for Your Trip

When planning your skiing or snowboarding trip to Colorado, it's essential to come prepared for the elements. Dress in warm, moisture-wicking layers to stay comfortable throughout the day. High-quality ski or snowboard equipment is key to a successful experience, so be sure to rent or bring your own gear. Most resorts offer rental services and have knowledgeable staff to help you find the right equipment. Additionally, helmets are recommended for safety, and eye protection such as goggles is a must to shield against sun glare and snow.

8.3 Whitewater Rafting and Kayaking

Whitewater rafting and kayaking in Colorado offer an amazing outdoor adventure that immerses visitors in the state's stunning river landscapes. Known for its majestic mountain ranges and powerful waterways, Colorado is a paradise for whitewater enthusiasts, offering a variety of river experiences that cater to all skill levels. From gentle floats to heart-pounding rapids, rafting and kayaking in Colorado provide an opportunity to explore the state's natural beauty in a truly unforgettable way.

The Power of the Rivers

Colorado's rivers are shaped by the melting snowpack from its towering mountains, creating a network of waterways that flow with energy and vitality. The Arkansas, Colorado, Animas, and Yampa rivers are among the most popular for whitewater rafting and kayaking, each offering its own unique character and challenges. The Arkansas River, one of the longest in the state, is renowned for its diverse range of rapids and beautiful scenery. From the thrilling Class IV and V rapids of the Royal Gorge to the family-friendly floats of Browns Canyon, the Arkansas River has something for everyone. The Colorado River, famous for its journey through the Grand Canyon, also offers excellent whitewater adventures in the state, particularly in the Glenwood Canyon section.

Thrilling Rapids and Calm Waters

Whitewater rafting and kayaking in Colorado allow visitors to experience a wide range of river conditions, from calm and serene stretches to adrenaline-pumping rapids. Picture yourself navigating the twists and turns of a rushing river, your raft bouncing over waves as you work together with your team to steer the boat. The thrill of the rapids is matched only by the sense of accomplishment when you conquer each challenge. For those seeking a more relaxed experience, many rivers offer gentle floats through picturesque canyons and lush valleys. You can take in the stunning scenery at a leisurely pace, enjoying the soothing sounds of the river and the chance to spot wildlife along the banks.

Expert Guides and Safety

Colorado's whitewater rafting and kayaking outfitters are known for their expertise and commitment to safety. When you book a guided trip, you'll be paired with experienced guides who provide valuable instruction and support throughout the journey. Whether you're a seasoned paddler or a first-timer, guides ensure you have the skills and knowledge needed to navigate the river safely. Before you embark on your adventure, your guide will provide a comprehensive safety briefing and equip you with all the necessary gear, including life jackets and helmets. Many outfitters also offer wetsuits or splash jackets to keep you warm in cooler water temperatures.

Bonding with Nature and Each Other

Whitewater rafting and kayaking are not just about the thrill of the rapids; they are also about connecting with nature and the people around you. As you float down the river, you'll have the chance to bond with your fellow adventurers, sharing laughs and stories along the way. The experience fosters a sense of camaraderie and teamwork as you navigate the river together. The natural beauty of Colorado's rivers is awe-inspiring, from towering cliffs and dense forests to vibrant wildflowers and cascading waterfalls. As you glide through this landscape, you'll gain a deeper appreciation for the state's pristine wilderness and the importance of preserving its natural resources.

Preparing for Your Adventure

When preparing for your whitewater rafting or kayaking adventure in Colorado, it's important to come equipped with the right clothing and gear. Dress in quick-drying, moisture-wicking clothing that will keep you comfortable whether you get splashed or stay dry. Water shoes or secure sandals are a must to protect your feet and provide traction. Be sure to bring sunscreen, sunglasses with a strap, and a hat to shield yourself from the sun. Many outfitters offer waterproof containers for your valuables, so you can keep them safe and dry during the trip.

8.4 Rock Climbing and Mountaineering

Rock climbing and mountaineering in Colorado offer an outdoor adventure that immerses visitors in the state's awe-inspiring mountain landscapes. Known for its jagged peaks and diverse rock formations, Colorado is a playground for climbers and mountaineers of all skill levels. Whether you're scaling the vertical walls of Eldorado Canyon, ascending one of the state's famous Fourteeners, or bouldering in the foothills, Colorado provides a unique and unforgettable experience for outdoor enthusiasts.

Climbing Destinations

Colorado is home to a wide variety of climbing destinations, each offering its own set of challenges and rewards. Eldorado Canyon, located just outside Boulder, is one of the state's most iconic climbing spots, known for its golden sandstone cliffs and classic multi-pitch routes. As you climb the walls of Eldorado Canyon, you'll be treated to breathtaking views of the surrounding valley and the distant peaks of the Rockies. In addition to traditional climbing areas, Colorado offers exceptional opportunities for bouldering, a form of rock climbing that focuses on short but intense routes close to the ground. Flagstaff Mountain and Horsetooth Reservoir are popular bouldering spots where you can test your strength and technique on a variety of rock formations.

Ascending the Fourteeners

Colorado boasts an impressive 58 peaks that rise over 14,000 feet, known as the Fourteeners. Climbing one of these majestic mountains is a rite of passage for many outdoor enthusiasts. The journey to the summit of a Fourteener often involves a mix of hiking, scrambling, and sometimes technical climbing, depending on the peak and route you choose. Mount Elbert, the highest peak in Colorado, offers a relatively straightforward ascent along its standard route, making it a great choice for beginners. For those seeking more technical challenges, peaks like Longs Peak or Capitol Peak provide exposed ridges and steep faces that require advanced climbing skills. The reward for reaching the summit of a Fourteener is unparalleled—a panoramic view of the surrounding mountains and valleys that stretches as far as the eye can see. It's a moment of triumph and a profound connection to the natural world.

Guided Climbs and Instruction

If you're new to rock climbing or mountaineering, Colorado offers a wealth of guided climbing experiences and instruction. Experienced guides can introduce you to the basics of climbing, from belaying and knot-tying to route selection and safety. They can also take you on more advanced climbs, sharing their knowledge of the terrain and providing support every step of the way. Guided climbs are a great way to explore the state's diverse climbing areas while learning from the experts. Many climbing schools and guide services offer customized trips based on your skill level and interests.

Embracing the Climbing Community

Rock climbing and mountaineering in Colorado provide an opportunity to connect with a vibrant and welcoming community of climbers. Whether you're climbing with friends, family, or joining a group, the sense of camaraderie and mutual support is a defining aspect of the climbing experience. Climbers often gather at local crags and climbing gyms, sharing stories, tips, and encouragement. The climbing community in Colorado is passionate about preserving the natural environment and promoting sustainable climbing practices, such as minimizing impact on the rock and wildlife.

Preparing for Your Adventure
When preparing for your rock climbing or mountaineering adventure in Colorado, it's important to come equipped with the right gear and clothing. A good pair of climbing shoes is essential for gripping the rock, while a harness and helmet provide safety and protection. Depending on the type of climb, you may also need a rope, belay device, and other specialized equipment. Dressing in layers is key, as weather conditions in the mountains can change rapidly. Bring plenty of water and snacks to stay hydrated and energized during the climb. Additionally, familiarize yourself with Leave No Trace principles to help protect the natural beauty of the area.

8.5 Wildlife Watching and Nature Tours
Wildlife watching and nature tours in Colorado offer an outdoor adventure that immerses visitors in the state's diverse ecosystems and stunning natural landscapes. With its sprawling national parks, lush forests, alpine meadows, and sweeping grasslands, Colorado is home to an abundance of wildlife and plant species. Whether

you're hiking through Rocky Mountain National Park, exploring the plains, or venturing into the backcountry, the opportunity to witness the wonders of nature up close is an unforgettable experience.

The Diversity of Colorado's Ecosystems

Colorado's geography is defined by its diverse landscapes, from the towering peaks of the Rocky Mountains to the wide open spaces of the eastern plains. These varied environments provide habitats for a rich variety of wildlife, from large mammals like elk and bison to a vast array of bird species and smaller animals. In the mountains, you might encounter elk grazing in alpine meadows, mule deer darting through aspen groves, or black bears foraging in dense forests. The Rocky Mountains are also home to mountain goats and bighorn sheep, often seen scaling steep cliffs with ease. For bird watchers, the mountains offer the chance to spot golden eagles, peregrine falcons, and ptarmigans.

National Parks and Wildlife Refuges

Colorado's national parks and wildlife refuges are some of the best places to experience the state's natural beauty and observe wildlife. Rocky Mountain National Park is a prime destination for nature lovers, with over 415 square miles of pristine wilderness and a network of trails that lead you through varied landscapes. As you hike through the park, you may encounter moose near a tranquil lake, hear the haunting call of a distant coyote, or catch a glimpse of a mountain lion in the shadows. Great Sand Dunes National Park and Preserve offers a unique experience with its towering sand dunes set against a backdrop of snow-capped mountains. The park is home to diverse wildlife, including pronghorns and kangaroo rats that have adapted to the sandy environment. The nearby wetlands provide habitat for migratory birds, making it a birdwatcher's paradise.

Exploring the Plains and Grasslands

The eastern plains of Colorado provide a different but equally captivating wildlife watching experience. These vast open spaces are home to herds of bison, pronghorns, and coyotes. In Pawnee National Grassland, you can witness prairie dogs popping out of their burrows or hear the distinctive call of a meadowlark. The grasslands are also an important habitat for raptors such as hawks and eagles, which can often be seen soaring overhead.

Guided Nature Tours and Experiences

Guided nature tours are a fantastic way to explore Colorado's wildlife and natural beauty. Knowledgeable guides can provide insights into the local flora and fauna, share stories about the region's ecology, and help you spot wildlife that you might otherwise miss. Many tour companies offer specialized experiences such as bird watching tours, wildlife safaris, and backcountry hikes. In addition to land-based tours, Colorado's rivers provide opportunities for wildlife watching from the water. Rafting or kayaking down the Colorado River or the Arkansas River can give you a unique perspective on the state's wildlife, including beavers, river otters, and a variety of waterfowl.

Tips for a Successful Wildlife Watching Adventure

When planning your wildlife watching and nature tour in Colorado, it's important to be prepared for a successful and respectful experience. Here are some considerations to keep in mind:

Binoculars and Camera: Bring a good pair of binoculars to observe wildlife from a safe distance and a camera to capture the beauty of the natural world.

Dress Appropriately: Dress in layers for changing weather conditions and wear comfortable, sturdy footwear for hiking and exploring.

Be Patient and Observant: Wildlife watching requires patience and a keen eye. Spend time quietly observing your surroundings and listening for signs of wildlife.

Respect Wildlife: Always maintain a safe distance from animals and avoid disturbing their natural behaviors. Follow any guidelines or rules provided by your guide or park staff.

Stay on Trails: When exploring nature, stick to designated trails to minimize impact on the environment and reduce the risk of disturbing wildlife.

CHAPTER 9
SHOPPING IN COLORADO

Click the link or Scan QR Code with a device to view a comprehensive map of Shopping Options in Colorado – https://shorturl.at/BPQ56

9.1 Souvenirs and Gifts

Shopping in Colorado for souvenirs and gifts is an experience that blends the state's rich history and culture with unique artisanal offerings. Whether you're looking for handcrafted jewelry, local food products, or art inspired by the Rocky Mountains, Colorado has a wealth of options to choose from. Shopping in Colorado is not only an opportunity to take home a special piece of the state's heritage but also to support local artisans and businesses. Let's explore the vibrant world of shopping for souvenirs and gifts in Colorado.

Local Art and Craftsmanship

Colorado is home to a thriving community of artists and craftspeople who draw inspiration from the state's natural beauty and cultural heritage. In many small towns and mountain communities, you'll find galleries and boutiques showcasing one-of-a-kind pieces, from intricate pottery and handcrafted glasswork to unique sculptures and paintings. For a taste of the Southwest, Native American art and jewelry are also available, reflecting the region's deep indigenous heritage. Many shops offer turquoise and silver jewelry, pottery, and woven textiles that capture the spirit of the region.

Culinary Delights and Local Products
When it comes to culinary gifts, Colorado offers a range of delicious options that make for memorable souvenirs. Local food products such as artisanal cheeses, honey, and jams can be found in specialty shops and farmers' markets. Colorado's craft beer scene is also renowned, with local breweries producing a wide variety of unique and flavorful brews that make for great gifts. For those with a sweet tooth, you can indulge in handmade chocolates, caramels, and other treats crafted by local confectioners. Colorado's high-altitude coffee is another popular option, offering a rich and smooth flavor that makes for a perfect gift for coffee enthusiasts.

Outdoor-Inspired Apparel and Gear
Given Colorado's outdoor adventure culture, many shops offer clothing and gear inspired by the state's rugged landscapes. Outdoor apparel brands based in Colorado often create high-quality, functional, and stylish clothing and accessories perfect for hiking, skiing, or simply enjoying the great outdoors.

You can also find unique apparel featuring designs inspired by Colorado's wildlife and scenery, from T-shirts and hats to jackets and accessories. These items make for great gifts that allow you to take a piece of Colorado's natural beauty with you.

Boutiques and Shopping Districts

Colorado's cities and towns boast vibrant shopping districts where you can explore a mix of local boutiques and well-known retailers. In Denver, the historic Larimer Square and the upscale Cherry Creek Shopping Center offer an array of shops where you can find unique gifts and souvenirs. In Boulder, Pearl Street Mall is a pedestrian-friendly shopping district known for its lively atmosphere and eclectic mix of shops. Steamboat Springs and Telluride are also home to charming shopping areas with specialty stores offering a wide range of locally made products.

9.2 Local Art and Craft Markets

Colorado is a haven for art and craft enthusiasts, offering a vibrant scene of local markets that celebrate the state's diverse and talented artisans. From bustling urban markets to quaint mountain town fairs, visitors can find unique, handmade treasures that capture the essence of Colorado's culture and natural beauty. These markets are more than just shopping destinations; they provide a chance to connect with local creators and immerse yourself in the community. Let's explore some of the most notable local art and craft markets in Colorado and what you can expect when you visit them.

Denver's RiNo Art District

The River North (RiNo) Art District in Denver is a hub for creativity, boasting a mix of art galleries, studios, and craft markets. On the first Friday of each month, RiNo hosts an art walk where visitors can explore the area's eclectic collection of art and crafts. Local artists open their studios to the public, showcasing their work and offering a behind-the-scenes look at their creative process. In addition to the art walk, the district is home to a variety of shops and markets featuring locally made goods. The Source Market Hall is a popular destination, offering an array of artisanal food products, crafts, and more. RiNo is also known for its stunning street art, adding to the district's vibrant and dynamic atmosphere.

Boulder Farmers' Market

The Boulder Farmers' Market is a beloved local market that takes place in downtown Boulder every Saturday and Wednesday during the warmer months. In addition to fresh produce and food vendors, the market features an array of local crafts, including pottery, jewelry, textiles, and woodworking. The market is a lively gathering place where you can interact with local artisans and support small businesses. Located near Boulder Creek, the market offers a picturesque setting for a leisurely stroll and shopping experience. Visitors can enjoy live music and sample delicious local treats while browsing the market's diverse offerings.

Old Colorado City Farmers' Market

Located in Colorado Springs, the Old Colorado City Farmers' Market is a charming market that features local art, crafts, and food products. The market is held on Saturdays from May through October and offers a variety of handmade goods, including candles, soaps, and handcrafted jewelry. The market is situated in the historic district of Old Colorado City, adding to its appeal with its beautiful architecture and quaint atmosphere. It's a great place to explore local creativity and find unique souvenirs to take home.

Art on the Streets in Pueblo

Pueblo's Art on the Streets is an annual public art exhibition that brings together local and regional artists to showcase their work in the city's downtown area. While not a traditional market, Art on the Streets features sculptures, installations, and murals that transform the streets into an open-air gallery. Visitors can take a self-guided tour to admire the art and learn about the artists behind each piece. The event runs from June to May each year, allowing plenty of time to explore the art and experience Pueblo's vibrant arts scene. In addition to the public art, visitors can also find local craft shops and boutiques offering unique handmade goods.

Durango's Local Art Markets

Durango, nestled in the southwest corner of Colorado, is known for its thriving arts community and local markets. The Durango Farmers' Market takes place on Saturdays from May to October, featuring local crafts alongside fresh produce and food products. Visitors can browse a selection of handmade jewelry, pottery, and textiles crafted by talented local artists. In addition to the farmers' market, Durango hosts seasonal craft fairs and events, such as the Durango Autumn Arts Festival. These events provide an opportunity to discover new artists and artisans while enjoying the town's scenic mountain backdrop.

9.3 Fashion and Apparel Boutiques

Colorado is home to a thriving fashion scene with a variety of boutiques offering stylish and unique apparel. From chic urban shops in Denver to cozy mountain boutiques in smaller towns, there's something for every fashion enthusiast to discover. These boutiques showcase a range of styles, from contemporary designs to Western-inspired pieces, often incorporating the state's love for outdoor adventure and natural beauty. Here's a look at some of Colorado's standout fashion and apparel boutiques and what you can expect when you visit them.

Exploring Denver's Fashion Districts

Denver's fashion scene is centered around vibrant districts like LoHi (Lower Highlands), RiNo (River North), and Cherry Creek North. These areas are known for their trendy boutiques offering curated collections of clothing, accessories, and footwear. Many of the shops prioritize local and sustainable fashion, featuring Colorado designers and brands. In LoHi, you'll find boutiques that blend urban style with outdoor flair, offering comfortable yet fashionable clothing perfect for Colorado's active lifestyle. RiNo's boutiques often feature a mix of streetwear, avant-garde designs, and vintage finds. Cherry Creek North, on the other hand, is home to upscale boutiques that offer high-end fashion and luxury brands.

Boulder's Pearl Street Mall

Boulder's Pearl Street Mall is a pedestrian-friendly shopping district known for its eclectic mix of boutiques, including several fashion and apparel shops. These boutiques cater to a diverse range of styles, from bohemian chic to sophisticated elegance. Many of the shops emphasize sustainable and ethically sourced fashion, reflecting Boulder's progressive and environmentally conscious community. As you stroll down Pearl Street, you'll find boutiques with carefully curated selections of clothing, jewelry, and accessories. Some shops focus on outdoor and activewear, while others offer stylish everyday apparel. The lively atmosphere of Pearl Street Mall, with its street performers and vibrant art scene, adds to the overall shopping experience.

Mountain Style in Aspen

Aspen is a renowned mountain town known for its luxurious ski resorts and high-end shopping scene. The town's fashion boutiques offer a mix of contemporary designs, upscale winter wear, and elegant evening attire. Whether you're looking for designer labels or unique, locally made pieces, Aspen's boutiques provide a sophisticated shopping experience. In addition to clothing, Aspen's boutiques often feature accessories like hats, scarves, and gloves that are perfect for the colder mountain climate. The town's scenic setting and upscale ambiance make shopping in Aspen a memorable experience.

Artistic Flair in Telluride

Telluride is a picturesque mountain town that combines natural beauty with artistic inspiration. The town's boutiques reflect this unique blend, offering fashion-forward designs with a touch of Western charm. From cozy sweaters and stylish outerwear to flowing dresses and chic accessories, Telluride's boutiques provide a range of options for fashion-conscious visitors. The town's compact and walkable layout makes it easy to explore the local shops, many of which are located along Colorado Avenue. As you browse the boutiques, you'll find pieces that capture the essence of Telluride's mountain lifestyle.

Unique Finds in Durango

Durango's fashion boutiques offer a laid-back, Southwestern-inspired shopping experience. The town's shops feature clothing and accessories that blend casual comfort with style, often incorporating earthy tones and natural fabrics. Many boutiques showcase locally made items, including handmade jewelry and artisanal accessories. Downtown Durango is the heart of the town's shopping scene, with boutiques located along Main Avenue and nearby streets. As you explore the shops, you'll find a mix of contemporary fashion, Western wear, and outdoor apparel.

The town's friendly atmosphere and historic charm add to the enjoyment of shopping in Durango.

9.4 Antique Shops and Vintage Finds

Exploring the vibrant world of antique shops and vintage finds in Colorado offers an adventure into the state's rich history and diverse cultural heritage. From historic downtown districts to eclectic neighborhoods, Colorado's antique stores offer a treasure trove of unique goods, ranging from vintage furniture and jewelry to rare books and collectible memorabilia.

Whispering Willows Antique Shop in Denver

Whispering Willows Antique Shop, located in Denver's historic South Broadway district, is known for its eclectic array of vintage furniture, art, and home decor. The shop is housed in a charming Victorian-style building, lending an air of nostalgia to the shopping experience. Visitors will find an impressive selection of antique clocks, ornate mirrors, and intricate glassware, as well as rare books and collectibles. The shop's knowledgeable staff is always on hand to provide guidance and share stories about the unique pieces on display. Parking is available nearby, making it convenient for visitors to explore the area.

Pioneer Treasures in Colorado Springs

Situated in the bustling Old Colorado City, Pioneer Treasures is a delightful destination for antique enthusiasts. The shop boasts an impressive assortment of vintage jewelry, collectibles, and rustic furniture, as well as an array of quirky, one-of-a-kind finds. Visitors can explore the store's curated displays and discover items such as antique toys, vintage records, and historic photographs. The shop's welcoming ambiance and friendly staff make it a favorite among locals and tourists alike. Easy access to nearby restaurants and cafes allows visitors to enjoy a full day of shopping and dining in the area.

Aspen Antiques in Aspen
Nestled in the picturesque town of Aspen, Aspen Antiques offers a curated selection of fine art, antique furniture, and exquisite jewelry. The shop's elegant interior and tasteful displays create a sophisticated shopping experience for visitors. Those in search of timeless pieces will be delighted by the shop's collection of vintage rugs, classic paintings, and handcrafted wooden furniture. Aspen Antiques is conveniently located in the heart of downtown Aspen, making it easy for visitors to explore the town's other attractions and enjoy a leisurely stroll through its scenic streets.

Fort Collins Emporium in Fort Collins
Fort Collins Emporium, located in the vibrant downtown district of Fort Collins, is a haven for collectors and antique lovers alike. The store features a wide range of vintage and antique goods, including furniture, home decor, and collectibles. Shoppers can browse through the aisles and discover treasures such as antique kitchenware, retro electronics, and unique art pieces. The emporium's central location allows visitors to explore nearby shops

and restaurants, making it a perfect destination for a day of leisurely shopping and dining.

Golden Gallery Antiques in Golden

Golden Gallery Antiques, located in the historic town of Golden, is a must-visit destination for those seeking rare and exquisite finds. The shop is known for its extensive collection of antique clocks, fine china, and delicate glassware. Visitors can peruse the store's carefully curated displays, which also include vintage jewelry and art pieces from different eras. The shop's charming location in the heart of Golden adds to the overall experience, allowing visitors to explore the town's historic sites and enjoy a scenic walk along Clear Creek.

9.5 Specialty Stores and Unique Finds

Colorado is known for its breathtaking landscapes, outdoor adventures, and rich cultural heritage, but the state also offers a wide array of specialty shops and unique finds that cater to a variety of tastes and interests. These shops offer visitors the chance to discover one-of-a-kind goods and products that reflect the local flavor and charm of Colorado.

The Spice Trader in Boulder

Located in the vibrant downtown area of Boulder, The Spice Trader is a specialty shop that caters to culinary enthusiasts and lovers of global flavors. The shop offers an extensive selection of spices, herbs, and gourmet ingredients from around the world.

Visitors can explore the beautifully organized shelves, discovering exotic blends, rare spices, and high-quality teas. The shop's knowledgeable staff provides expert advice on flavor pairings and cooking techniques, making it a favorite destination for home cooks and professional chefs alike. The Spice Trader's central location allows visitors to easily explore Boulder's eclectic shopping district and enjoy a variety of dining options.

The Green Collective in Fort Collins
The Green Collective in Fort Collins is a specialty shop dedicated to sustainable and eco-friendly products. Situated in the historic Old Town district, the shop offers a curated selection of zero-waste and ethically sourced goods, including reusable household items, organic skincare products, and eco-conscious fashion. Visitors can browse the shop's thoughtfully designed displays, learning about the environmental impact of their purchases and how to make greener choices. The shop's commitment to sustainability resonates with the environmentally conscious community in Fort Collins and beyond. Nearby parking and bike-friendly paths make it easy for visitors to access the store.

Wild Iris Boutique in Durango
In the charming town of Durango, Wild Iris Boutique is a specialty shop that focuses on artisanal jewelry, handcrafted accessories, and unique fashion pieces. The boutique's elegant interior and warm ambiance create a welcoming shopping experience for visitors. Shoppers can discover locally made jewelry featuring

precious stones and metals, as well as stylish clothing and accessories from independent designers. Wild Iris Boutique's prime location in downtown Durango makes it an ideal stop for visitors exploring the area's historic sites and scenic attractions.

The Cheese Importers in Longmont

The Cheese Importers in Longmont is a specialty shop that delights cheese lovers with its impressive selection of international and domestic cheeses. The shop is located in a renovated warehouse, creating a charming and rustic atmosphere. Visitors can explore the walk-in cheese cave, stocked with a variety of artisanal cheeses from around the world. In addition to cheese, the shop offers a selection of gourmet foods, including cured meats, specialty oils, and vinegars. The attached French bistro provides a delightful dining experience, allowing visitors to enjoy a meal after shopping. The shop's location offers ample parking, making it easily accessible for visitors.

BookBar in Denver

BookBar in Denver is a unique concept that combines a cozy bookstore with a welcoming wine bar. Located in the Tennyson Street district, the shop offers a curated selection of books across various genres, as well as a carefully chosen list of wines and craft beers. Visitors can peruse the shelves for literary treasures while enjoying a glass of wine or a cup of coffee. The shop's inviting atmosphere encourages relaxation and conversation, making it a popular spot for book lovers and social gatherings.

CHAPTER 10

DAY TRIPS AND EXCURSIONS

10.1 Nearby Towns and Villages

Embarking on a day trip to one of Colorado's charming villages or towns is a delightful way to experience the state's natural beauty, rich history, and warm hospitality. Whether you are looking to stroll through quaint streets, take in picturesque mountain views, or immerse yourself in local culture, there is a destination in Colorado that will cater to your desires. Let's explore some of the most captivating villages and towns in Colorado that make for memorable day trips.

Georgetown:

Situated in a valley surrounded by towering peaks, the historic town of Georgetown offers a glimpse into Colorado's mining past. Located just off Interstate 70, approximately 45 miles west of

Denver, Georgetown is easily accessible by car. The town's well-preserved Victorian architecture adds to its old-world charm, inviting visitors to take a leisurely stroll down its main street lined with antique shops and cozy cafes. A must-do activity in Georgetown is a ride on the Georgetown Loop Railroad, a scenic train journey that winds through the Rocky Mountains and over a series of breathtaking bridges. For history enthusiasts, the Hotel de Paris Museum offers a fascinating look at the town's history and the Gold Rush era. Don't forget to visit nearby Silver Plume, a quaint neighboring town, for even more historic sites and scenic views.

Crested Butte:

Crested Butte is a picturesque mountain town located in the Gunnison Valley in southwestern Colorado. Known for its colorful Victorian homes and vibrant wildflower displays, the town exudes a lively, artistic atmosphere. To get there, visitors can take US Highway 50 west from Gunnison and then head north on CO-135. Outdoor enthusiasts will find plenty to do in Crested Butte, from hiking and mountain biking in the summer to skiing and snowboarding in the winter. The town's main street is lined with boutique shops, art galleries, and eateries offering farm-to-table cuisine. The annual Crested Butte Wildflower Festival in July is a must-see event, attracting nature lovers from all over to witness the breathtaking blooms.

Estes Park:

Situated at the eastern entrance to Rocky Mountain National Park, Estes Park is a popular destination for visitors seeking outdoor adventures and stunning mountain views. The town is about 70 miles northwest of Denver and can be reached via US Highway 36. In Estes Park, visitors can explore the town's charming downtown area, filled with shops, restaurants, and galleries. A highlight of the town is the iconic Stanley Hotel, known for its grand architecture and historical significance as the inspiration for Stephen King's The Shining. Outdoor activities abound, including hiking, wildlife watching, and taking a scenic drive along Trail Ridge Road in Rocky Mountain National Park.

Manitou Springs:

Manitou Springs, located just west of Colorado Springs, is a bohemian mountain town known for its artsy vibe and natural mineral springs. The town can be reached via US Highway 24, making it a convenient day trip from Colorado Springs. Visitors can enjoy strolling through the town's vibrant streets, discovering unique boutiques, art galleries, and inviting cafes. The nearby Garden of the Gods offers breathtaking red rock formations and hiking trails. For those looking for a challenge, the Manitou Incline is a steep hike with rewarding views at the top. Additionally, visitors can relax in the healing waters of the town's natural mineral springs.

Paonia:

Paonia, located in the North Fork Valley on the western slope of Colorado, is a small town known for its orchards, vineyards, and local produce. The town can be reached via CO-92, offering a scenic drive through the mountains. Visitors can tour local farms and vineyards, tasting fresh fruit and locally produced wines. The town's close-knit community hosts several festivals throughout the year, such as the Paonia Cherry Days and the Mountain Harvest Festival, celebrating the region's agricultural heritage. Outdoor enthusiasts can also explore nearby areas like the West Elk Wilderness and the North Fork Gunnison River.

10.2 National Parks and Recreation Areas

Colorado's breathtaking landscapes offer a wealth of opportunities for day trips to national parks and recreational areas. The state's diverse terrain, ranging from towering mountain peaks to lush forests and arid desert canyons, provides an ideal setting for outdoor adventures and memorable experiences. Let's explore some of the most captivating national parks and recreational areas in Colorado that make for unforgettable day trips.

Rocky Mountain National Park:

Rocky Mountain National Park, located about 70 miles northwest of Denver, is one of Colorado's most iconic natural treasures. To reach the park, visitors can take US Highway 34 or US Highway 36 from the nearby town of Estes Park. The park encompasses over 415 square miles of stunning alpine scenery, with soaring peaks, lush valleys, and pristine lakes. Visitors can drive along Trail Ridge Road, one of the highest paved roads in the United States, offering panoramic views of the surrounding mountains and valleys. Hiking enthusiasts can choose from a variety of trails, ranging from easy strolls around Bear Lake to challenging treks up Longs Peak. Wildlife lovers will have the chance to spot elk, moose, and bighorn sheep in their natural habitats. Camping, fishing, and horseback riding are also popular activities in the park.

Great Sand Dunes National Park and Preserve:

Great Sand Dunes National Park and Preserve is located in the San Luis Valley, about 240 miles south of Denver. To get there, visitors can take US Highway 160 to Colorado State Highway 150. This unique park is home to North America's tallest sand dunes, set against the backdrop of the snow-capped Sangre de Cristo Mountains. Exploring the dunes is a must-do activity, whether by hiking to the summit of Star Dune, sandboarding down the slopes, or simply enjoying the mesmerizing landscape. The park also features the Medano Creek, which flows seasonally and provides a refreshing place to splash and play. Visitors can take advantage of nearby camping areas or enjoy a picnic with stunning views of the dunes and mountains.

Black Canyon of the Gunnison National Park:

Black Canyon of the Gunnison National Park is situated in western Colorado, about 250 miles southwest of Denver. The park can be reached via US Highway 50, with the South Rim entrance near

Montrose and the North Rim entrance near Crawford. This park is known for its awe-inspiring black granite cliffs and steep, narrow canyon. Visitors can explore the park's scenic drives, such as the South Rim Drive, which offers breathtaking viewpoints overlooking the canyon. Hiking trails range from easy walks along the rim to challenging descents into the canyon itself. The park is a haven for rock climbers, and the Gunnison River is renowned for its excellent fishing and white-water rafting opportunities.

Mesa Verde National Park:

Mesa Verde National Park, located in southwestern Colorado, is a UNESCO World Heritage Site and one of the most important archaeological sites in the United States. To get there, visitors can take US Highway 160 and follow the signs to the park entrance near the town of Mancos. The park preserves the ancient cliff dwellings of the Ancestral Pueblo people, offering a glimpse into their fascinating history and culture. Guided tours allow visitors to explore iconic sites such as Cliff Palace and Balcony House, where they can marvel at the intricate stone structures built into the canyon walls. The park also features a visitor center with exhibits on the region's archaeology and history. The surrounding area offers additional hiking opportunities and beautiful views of the canyons and mesas.

Maroon Bells-Snowmass:

The Maroon Bells-Snowmass Wilderness, located near Aspen in the Elk Mountains, is a breathtaking area known for its iconic peaks, pristine lakes, and dense forests. To access the area, visitors can take CO-82 to Maroon Creek Road, which leads to the Maroon Bells Scenic Area. A bus service operates during peak seasons to reduce traffic and protect the environment. The Maroon Bells are two of the most photographed mountains in Colorado, and their reflection in Maroon Lake creates a postcard-perfect scene. Hiking trails abound, from easy walks around the lake to more challenging routes that take visitors deep into the wilderness. This area is also popular for fishing, camping, and wildlife viewing, making it a serene escape into nature.

10.3 Scenic Drives and Road Trips

Taking a scenic drive or embarking on a road trip through Colorado is a magical way to experience the state's diverse landscapes and natural beauty. From breathtaking mountain passes to serene byways that wind through forests and canyons, Colorado's roads offer unparalleled views and memorable adventures. Here, we'll explore some of the most captivating drives and road trips in Colorado, each with its own unique charm and vistas.

Trail Ridge Road:

Trail Ridge Road is one of Colorado's most iconic drives, taking travelers through Rocky Mountain National Park from Estes Park to Grand Lake. Known as the "Highway to the Sky," this road reaches elevations of over 12,000 feet, providing awe-inspiring views of snow-capped peaks, alpine tundra, and pristine valleys. As you wind your way along the road, keep an eye out for wildlife such as elk and marmots. There are numerous pull-offs and viewpoints where you can stop to take photos and breathe in the crisp mountain air. Be prepared for changing weather conditions, as the high altitudes can bring sudden storms or snow, even in summer.

San Juan Skyway:

The San Juan Skyway is a 236-mile loop that winds through southwestern Colorado, showcasing the state's rugged San Juan Mountains. The route takes you through historic mining towns such as Durango, Silverton, and Ouray, each with its own unique charm and character. As you drive, you'll encounter dramatic mountain passes, lush forests, and picturesque valleys. The Million Dollar Highway section of the drive between Ouray and Silverton is known for its steep, winding roads and breathtaking views. Along the way, you can explore old mining sites, hot springs, and enjoy outdoor activities such as hiking and fishing.

Peak to Peak Scenic Byway:

The Peak to Peak Scenic Byway stretches from Estes Park to Central City, taking travelers on a 55-mile journey through the northern Front Range of the Rocky Mountains. This drive offers sweeping views of mountain peaks, dense forests, and charming mountain towns. In Estes Park, you can visit the iconic Stanley Hotel or take a detour into Rocky Mountain National Park. As you continue south, you'll pass through the artsy town of Nederland and the historic mining town of Central City, where you can try your luck at the casinos or enjoy a meal in one of the town's cozy eateries.

Mount Evans Scenic Byway:

Mount Evans Scenic Byway takes you to the summit of Mount Evans, one of Colorado's famous 14,000-foot peaks. The drive starts in Idaho Springs and winds its way up to the summit, offering panoramic views of the surrounding mountains and valleys. The byway is the highest paved road in North America, and the journey to the top is an unforgettable experience. Along the way, you'll pass through different ecological zones, from pine forests to alpine tundra. Once you reach the summit, you can explore the ruins of Crest House and hike to the nearby peak for stunning views.

Dinosaur Diamond Prehistoric Highway:

The Dinosaur Diamond Prehistoric Highway is a 480-mile loop that takes travelers through the ancient history of Colorado and Utah. The drive includes stops at several national monuments, including Dinosaur National Monument, known for its impressive fossil beds. The highway passes through the towns of Grand Junction, Fruita, and Rifle in Colorado, each offering its own attractions and unique landscapes. In Fruita, you can visit the Colorado National Monument for breathtaking views of red rock canyons and mesas. The journey provides a fascinating glimpse into the prehistoric past and the geological wonders of the region.

10.4 Adventure Tours and Excursions

Colorado is a playground for adventure seekers, offering an array of tours and excursions that allow visitors to immerse themselves in the state's stunning natural beauty and exhilarating outdoor activities. Whether you're drawn to the thrill of white-water rafting, the rush of mountain biking, or the awe of exploring deep canyons, there's an adventure in Colorado waiting for you. Let's delve into some of the most exciting adventure tours and excursions the state has to offer and the experiences that await you.

White-Water Rafting on the Arkansas River

The Arkansas River is one of Colorado's most popular destinations for white-water rafting, offering thrilling rapids and breathtaking scenery. The river winds its way through the heart of the Rocky Mountains, providing a range of rafting experiences suitable for different skill levels. For those new to the sport, the stretches near Buena Vista and Salida offer gentle rapids and beautiful mountain views. More experienced rafters can tackle the challenging sections of the river, such as the Royal Gorge, known for its intense Class III to V rapids. Numerous outfitters in the area provide guided rafting tours, ensuring a safe and exciting experience. These tours typically include safety instructions, all necessary equipment, and knowledgeable guides who share their expertise about the river and surrounding landscape. Rafting on the Arkansas River is a thrilling way to connect with nature and experience the power of the river.

Hiking Within the Maroon Bells-Snowmass Wilderness

The Maroon Bells-Snowmass Wilderness is a hiker's paradise, with its iconic peaks, pristine lakes, and lush forests offering a wide variety of trails for all skill levels. Located near Aspen, the wilderness area is home to the famous Maroon Bells, two stunning peaks that rise majestically above Maroon Lake. Visitors can choose from numerous hiking trails, such as the easy loop around Maroon Lake, which provides stunning views of the mountains and reflections in the water. For those seeking a more challenging adventure, the hike to Crater Lake offers rugged terrain and breathtaking vistas. During peak season, a shuttle service is available from Aspen to the Maroon Bells Scenic Area, ensuring easy access while protecting the environment.

Jeep Tours in Ouray

Ouray, often referred to as the "Switzerland of America," is nestled in the San Juan Mountains and offers a variety of off-road adventures for thrill-seekers. Jeep tours are a popular way to explore the rugged terrain and historic mining sites that surround the town. Guided tours take visitors along old mining roads, such as the famous Imogene Pass and Engineer Pass, offering panoramic views of the mountains, wildflowers, and abandoned mines. The knowledgeable guides share stories of the region's rich history and geology, adding depth to the experience. These tours are suitable for all ages and provide an exciting way to see areas of Colorado that are otherwise inaccessible.

Ziplining in Colorado Springs

For those who crave an adrenaline rush, ziplining in Colorado Springs offers a thrilling experience high above the ground. Several zipline parks in the area provide courses with varying levels of difficulty, allowing visitors to soar through the trees and take in stunning views of the surrounding mountains. One popular destination for ziplining is the Broadmoor Seven Falls area, where visitors can experience a series of ziplines that traverse the canyon and offer breathtaking views of the falls. The parks provide all necessary safety equipment and professional guides to ensure a safe and exhilarating adventure.

Canyoning in the Black Canyon of the Gunnison

The Black Canyon of the Gunnison National Park is known for its dramatic cliffs and steep canyons, making it a prime location for canyoning adventures. Canyoning, also known as canyoneering, involves exploring canyons by hiking, climbing, and sometimes rappelling down waterfalls. Guided canyoning tours in the park offer a thrilling way to experience the rugged beauty of the canyon. Visitors can explore remote areas that are otherwise difficult to access, immersing themselves in the natural wonders of the park. The tours include safety gear and expert guides who provide instructions on navigating the challenging terrain.

Colorado's adventure tours and excursions provide endless opportunities to explore the state's natural wonders while pushing your limits and trying something new. Whether you're seeking the thrill of rafting, the challenge of hiking, or the excitement of ziplining, Colorado's outdoor adventures offer unforgettable experiences that will leave you with memories to cherish for a lifetime.

10.5 Family-Friendly Day Outings

Colorado is a haven for families, offering an abundance of activities that cater to kids and adults alike. The state's natural beauty and vibrant culture provide endless opportunities for memorable outings and educational experiences. From outdoor adventures to interactive museums, there is something for everyone in the family to enjoy. Here's a closer look at some of the best family-friendly activities in Colorado, each offering a unique experience that will leave lasting memories.

Exploring the Denver Museum of Nature & Science

The Denver Museum of Nature & Science is a must-visit destination for families. Located in Denver's City Park, the museum features a wide range of exhibits that engage visitors of all ages. Kids can marvel at the towering dinosaur skeletons, learn about the wonders of the natural world, and explore the mysteries of outer space in the planetarium. The museum also offers interactive exhibits, hands-on activities, and educational programs that bring science and nature to life. Special events and temporary exhibits throughout the year provide fresh experiences for returning visitors. A visit to the Denver Museum of Nature &

Science is both entertaining and educational, making it a perfect outing for families.

Adventuring in the Garden of the Gods

Garden of the Gods is a stunning natural park located in Colorado Springs, offering a captivating outdoor experience for families. The park is known for its towering red rock formations and scenic vistas, providing a perfect backdrop for a day of exploration. Families can enjoy easy hikes along well-maintained trails, such as the Perkins Central Garden Trail, which winds through the heart of the park and offers close-up views of the rock formations. The park also offers guided nature walks, rock climbing opportunities, and a visitor center with exhibits and interactive displays. The nearby Garden of the Gods Trading Post provides a place to shop for souvenirs and grab a bite to eat, making it a convenient stop during your visit. Whether you're taking a leisurely stroll or embarking on an adventure, Garden of the Gods is a family-friendly destination that showcases Colorado's natural beauty.

Visit the Cheyenne Mountain Zoo

The Cheyenne Mountain Zoo in Colorado Springs is a top attraction for families, offering a unique and memorable wildlife experience. Perched on the side of Cheyenne Mountain, the zoo provides breathtaking views of the surrounding area while you explore its many exhibits. Kids will love the opportunity to hand-feed giraffes and interact with other animals such as wallabies and penguins. The zoo features a wide variety of species, from big cats to primates, and even a carousel and playground for younger visitors. The zoo's commitment to conservation and education is evident in its exhibits and programs, making it both a fun and enriching experience for the whole family.

Discovering History at the Colorado Railroad Museum

Located in Golden, the Colorado Railroad Museum offers a fascinating journey through the state's rich railroad history. Families can explore the museum's extensive collection of vintage locomotives, passenger cars, and freight cars, many of which are open for visitors to step inside. The museum offers train rides on select weekends, allowing kids to experience the thrill of a ride on a historic steam locomotive. Interactive exhibits and displays provide insight into the role of railroads in shaping Colorado's history and development. The museum's outdoor picnic area is perfect for enjoying a family meal surrounded by the sights and sounds of the railroad.

Enjoying a Day at Elitch Gardens

Elitch Gardens is a popular amusement park located in Denver, offering a day of fun and excitement for families. The park features a variety of rides, from thrilling roller coasters to family-friendly attractions like the carousel and Ferris wheel. There is also a water park section with slides, wave pools, and splash areas for kids. In addition to rides, Elitch Gardens hosts live entertainment and special events throughout the season.

CHAPTER 11
ENTERTAINMENT AND NIGHTLIFE

11.1 Live Music Venues and Concerts

Colorado's music scene is as dynamic and diverse as its landscape, offering a variety of live music venues that cater to all tastes and styles. From intimate clubs to grand amphitheaters, music lovers will find a range of options to enjoy concerts and performances throughout the state. Whether you're drawn to the majestic beauty of Red Rocks or the cozy atmosphere of a local pub, Colorado's live music venues provide unforgettable experiences.

Red Rocks Amphitheatre:

Nestled within the stunning red rock formations of Morrison, Colorado, Red Rocks Amphitheatre is an iconic outdoor venue that draws music enthusiasts from around the world. The natural acoustics of the amphitheater, combined with its breathtaking setting, make it one of the most unique and memorable places to experience live music. Red Rocks hosts a diverse lineup of concerts throughout the year, featuring top artists from various genres, including rock, pop, country, and electronic. The venue's tiered seating provides excellent views of the stage and the surrounding landscape. Arrive early to explore the park's hiking trails or to catch a beautiful Colorado sunset before the show.

The Ogden Theatre:

Located on East Colfax Avenue in Denver, the Ogden Theatre is a historic music venue that has been a staple of the city's entertainment scene since 1917. The theater's ornate architecture and intimate atmosphere make it a popular destination for both artists and audiences. The Ogden Theatre hosts a wide range of concerts, from indie bands and up-and-coming artists to established acts from various genres. The venue's excellent acoustics and cozy seating ensure an engaging experience for concertgoers. Be sure to check the theater's schedule for upcoming shows and plan your visit accordingly.

The Bluebird Theater:

Another historic gem on Colfax Avenue, the Bluebird Theater is known for its vibrant blue neon sign and its role in Denver's live music scene. Since opening in 1919, the theater has hosted a variety of performances, including live music, comedy, and theater productions. The Bluebird Theater's intimate setting allows for a close connection between the audience and performers. The venue features a mix of local and touring acts across different genres, providing music lovers with a diverse array of shows to enjoy. Its prime location on one of Denver's busiest streets makes it easily accessible and surrounded by a variety of dining and nightlife options.

The Fox Theatre:

In the heart of Boulder, the Fox Theatre is a beloved live music venue that has been hosting performances since 1992. Known for its excellent sound quality and intimate setting, the Fox Theatre is a favorite among both artists and fans. The venue offers a diverse lineup of concerts, including rock, blues, jazz, and electronic music. The Fox Theatre's proximity to the University of Colorado Boulder and the vibrant Pearl Street Mall area adds to its appeal. Plan to explore the nearby shops and restaurants before or after the show for a complete Boulder experience.

Levitt Pavilion Denver:

For those seeking an outdoor music experience in Denver, Levitt Pavilion offers a series of free concerts throughout the summer. Located in Ruby Hill Park, the pavilion provides a picturesque setting with its grassy lawn and stage overlooking the city. Levitt Pavilion's mission is to bring music to the community by offering a wide variety of free concerts featuring local, national, and international artists across genres. Attendees can bring blankets, lawn chairs, and picnic baskets to enjoy a relaxing evening under the stars. Food trucks and vendors are also available on-site for refreshments.

11.2 Performing Arts and Theatrical Performances

Colorado's vibrant performing arts scene is a rich tapestry of theatrical performances, dance, music, and more. The state's diverse array of venues and productions cater to every taste, offering visitors the chance to experience world-class performances and local talent alike. Whether you find yourself in the bustling city of Denver or the scenic town of Aspen, there's no shortage of opportunities to enjoy the performing arts.

The Denver Center for the Performing Arts:

The Denver Center for the Performing Arts (DCPA) is one of the largest performing arts centers in the country, offering a wide variety of performances and events throughout the year. Located in downtown Denver, the DCPA comprises several theaters, including the Ellie Caulkins Opera House, Buell Theatre, and the Garner Galleria Theatre, each providing a unique experience. The DCPA's season includes Broadway shows, contemporary plays, opera, ballet, and comedy. Ticket prices vary depending on the performance and seating section, but the center often offers discounted tickets for students and military personnel. Visitors can catch an evening show and enjoy the vibrant atmosphere of downtown Denver's nightlife before or after the performance. The DCPA's theaters typically open an hour before showtime, with performance start times ranging from early evenings to later in the evening.

Colorado Ballet:

The Colorado Ballet is a professional ballet company based in Denver that offers captivating performances throughout its season. The company's repertoire includes classical ballets like Swan Lake and The Nutcracker, as well as contemporary works and world premieres. Performances take place at the Ellie Caulkins Opera House, known for its stunning architecture and intimate seating. Ticket prices vary depending on the production and seating, with discounts available for students and groups. The Colorado Ballet's schedule typically features evening shows during the week and matinee performances on weekends, making it easy to plan a visit around your schedule.

Boulder Theater:
The Boulder Theater is a historic venue located in the heart of downtown Boulder. Known for its Art Deco style and welcoming ambiance, the theater hosts a variety of live performances, including theater, music, dance, and comedy. The theater's schedule is always evolving, featuring local and national acts across a range of genres. Ticket prices are generally affordable, and the theater's intimate setting ensures an engaging experience for the audience. Before or after a show, visitors can explore Boulder's lively Pearl Street Mall area, filled with shops, restaurants, and street performers.

Aspen Music Festival and School:
The Aspen Music Festival and School is one of the world's leading classical music festivals, attracting musicians and audiences from around the globe. Located in the picturesque town of Aspen, the festival offers a summer season of concerts, recitals, and masterclasses, showcasing top talent in a beautiful mountain setting. Performances take place at various venues, including the

Benedict Music Tent and Harris Concert Hall. Ticket prices vary depending on the event, with options for both general admission and reserved seating. The festival's schedule is packed with events, from orchestral concerts to chamber music recitals, providing something for every music lover.

The Little Theatre of the Rockies:

The Little Theatre of the Rockies is a professional summer theater company based at the University of Northern Colorado in Greeley. The theater offers a season of productions featuring a mix of classic plays, musicals, and contemporary works. Performances take place at the Norton Theatre and the Langworthy Theatre on the university's campus. Ticket prices are affordable, making it an accessible option for families and students. The theater's summer season includes evening shows and occasional matinees, allowing visitors to enjoy a performance during their stay in northern Colorado.

11.3 Nightclubs and Dance Floors

Colorado's nightlife scene is as diverse and dynamic as the state's natural landscapes. Whether you're a fan of electronic dance music, hip-hop, Latin beats, or classic hits, you'll find a venue that suits your tastes. Colorado's clubs and dance floors offer a welcoming atmosphere, lively crowds, and top-notch DJs and performers. Here's an in-depth look at some of the best nightclubs and dance floors in Colorado, along with important information for visitors planning a night out.

Club Vinyl:

Located in the heart of Denver, Club Vinyl is one of the city's most popular nightclubs, offering a multi-level experience that caters to a variety of music tastes. The club features four distinct floors, each with its own music style and ambiance. From hip-hop and R&B to house and techno, there's something for everyone at Club Vinyl. The club is known for hosting top DJs and live performers from around the world. Prices for entry vary depending on the event and the night of the week, with some nights offering discounted or free admission before a certain time. Club Vinyl opens around 9:00 p.m. and closes in the early hours of the morning, typically around 2:00 a.m. It's a great spot to dance the night away and enjoy the city's vibrant nightlife.

Beta Nightclub:

Beta Nightclub is another top destination for nightlife in Denver, known for its cutting-edge sound system and focus on electronic dance music (EDM). The club features a spacious dance floor, state-of-the-art lighting, and world-class DJs who spin the latest tracks in EDM and techno. Beta Nightclub often hosts themed nights and special events, making each visit a unique experience. Entry prices vary depending on the event, and the club typically opens at 9:00 p.m. and closes around 2:00 a.m. Beta Nightclub's commitment to sustainability and environmental responsibility adds an extra layer of appeal for environmentally-conscious partygoers.

The Church Nightclub:

Housed in a historic church building, The Church Nightclub offers a one-of-a-kind nightlife experience in Denver. The venue features multiple rooms and dance floors, each with its own style and music genre. From the main room's high-energy dance floor to the rooftop patio with stunning views of the city, The Church Nightclub has something for every type of partygoer. The club often hosts themed parties and special events, drawing in a diverse and energetic crowd. Entry prices vary depending on the event, with discounted or free admission offered on certain nights. The Church Nightclub typically opens around 9:00 p.m. and closes around 2:00 a.m., giving you plenty of time to enjoy the night.

Whiskey Tango Foxtrot:

Located in downtown Denver, Whiskey Tango Foxtrot is a stylish nightclub that offers a blend of upscale ambiance and energetic dance floors. The club features a modern design, a spacious dance floor, and a rooftop patio with great views of the city. The music selection spans a variety of genres, including pop, hip-hop, and electronic. Whiskey Tango Foxtrot often hosts live bands and DJs, making each night a memorable experience. Entry prices vary depending on the event and night of the week, with some nights offering discounted admission. The club opens around 9:00 p.m. and closes around 2:00 a.m., providing a chic and sophisticated setting for a night out.

Mynt Lounge:

For those seeking a taste of Latin nightlife, Mynt Lounge in Denver is the place to be. This nightclub offers a vibrant atmosphere with Latin music, salsa dancing, and delicious cocktails. The dance floor is always packed with lively crowds moving to the beats of reggaeton, salsa, and merengue. Mynt Lounge often hosts special events and themed nights, making each visit a unique and exciting experience. Entry prices vary depending on the night, and the lounge typically opens around 9:00 p.m. and closes around 2:00 a.m. Whether you're a seasoned dancer or just looking to enjoy the lively atmosphere, Mynt Lounge is a must-visit for a night of Latin flair.

11.4 Comedy Clubs and Improv Shows

Colorado's comedy scene is a lively and welcoming community where you can experience the best of stand-up comedy and improv shows. Whether you're in the bustling city of Denver or one of the smaller towns throughout the state, there's no shortage of opportunities to laugh the night away. From local talent to nationally recognized comedians, Colorado's comedy clubs offer unforgettable evenings of entertainment.

Comedy Works:

Comedy Works is one of Denver's most iconic comedy clubs, known for its warm, intimate atmosphere and impressive lineup of top-notch comedians. The club has two locations in the city: Comedy Works Downtown in Larimer Square and Comedy Works

South at The Landmark in Greenwood Village. The downtown location is housed in the historic Writer's Square and offers an inviting, cozy setting for comedy shows. It's a great spot to catch nationally recognized comedians as well as up-and-coming talent. Comedy Works South features a more modern ambiance with a larger seating capacity, making it perfect for bigger shows. Both locations offer shows throughout the week, with prices varying depending on the performer and seating section. Comedy Works typically opens its doors an hour before showtime, with shows often starting around 7:30 or 8:00 p.m. Some nights offer multiple showtimes, giving you the flexibility to plan your visit around your schedule.

Improv Comedy Club:
Improv Comedy Club, located in Denver, is a popular venue that features a mix of stand-up comedy and improv shows. The club's cozy setting and talented lineup of performers create an engaging and lively experience for audiences. Improv Comedy Club hosts shows throughout the week, including open mic nights where local comedians can test their material. Ticket prices are generally affordable, making it an accessible option for a fun night out. The club opens its doors about an hour before showtime, which is typically around 7:30 or 8:00 p.m.

The Denver Improv:
The Denver Improv, located in the Stapleton neighborhood of Denver, is a popular destination for comedy lovers. This club

features a mix of stand-up comedy and improv shows, drawing talent from both the local scene and across the country. The venue's spacious seating and state-of-the-art sound and lighting systems make for a comfortable and enjoyable experience. Shows are held throughout the week, and ticket prices vary depending on the performer and seating section. The club usually opens its doors around an hour before showtime, with most shows starting in the evening.

Bovine Metropolis Theater:

For those seeking a night of pure improvisation, the Bovine Metropolis Theater in Denver is the place to be. This theater is dedicated to improv comedy and offers a wide range of shows, including long-form and short-form improv, sketch comedy, and improv classes. The intimate theater creates an engaging atmosphere, allowing audiences to feel like they're part of the performance. Bovine Metropolis Theater offers shows on weekends and select weekdays, with ticket prices generally being affordable. The theater's schedule can vary, so it's best to check their calendar for specific showtimes and details.

Loonees Comedy Corner:

Loonees Comedy Corner in Colorado Springs is a favorite among locals for its friendly atmosphere and quality comedy shows. The club features a mix of local and national comedians, providing a diverse lineup of performances. Loonees offers shows on Fridays and Saturdays, with additional shows on select nights. Ticket prices are generally reasonable, and the club usually opens its doors about an hour before showtime. The cozy setting ensures a close connection between the audience and performers, making for a memorable night of laughter.

11.5 Late-Night Eateries and Hangouts

When the sun goes down, Colorado comes alive with a variety of late-night eateries and hangout spots that cater to night owls looking for a bite to eat or a place to relax with friends. From cozy diners serving comfort food to trendy lounges offering craft cocktails, there's something for everyone in the Centennial State. Let's take a closer look at some of the top late-night spots across Colorado.

Snooze, an A.M. Eatery:

Snooze may be known for its breakfast and brunch, but many locations across Colorado offer extended hours for those who prefer breakfast for dinner. The Denver-based chain serves a variety of inventive and delicious dishes, such as pineapple upside-down pancakes, savory egg scrambles, and their signature "Benny" variations of eggs Benedict. Snooze has several locations in Denver, Boulder, Fort Collins, and other parts of Colorado, making it easily accessible for most residents and visitors. While most locations close by 2:30 p.m., you may find select locations open later for dinner or special events. Check their website for the latest updates on hours and availability.

Pete's Kitchen:

Located on East Colfax Avenue in Denver, Pete's Kitchen is a classic 24-hour diner that's been serving up hearty comfort food since 1942. This family-owned establishment offers a wide range of options, from all-day breakfast to classic Greek and American dishes. Whether you're craving a stack of pancakes, a gyro, or a patty melt, Pete's Kitchen has you covered. Prices are reasonable, making it a go-to spot for late-night cravings. The diner maintains a casual atmosphere and friendly service, making it a favorite hangout spot for locals and visitors alike.

Sassafras American Eatery:

For those seeking a taste of Southern comfort food in Denver, Sassafras American Eatery offers a cozy and welcoming atmosphere. Located on East Colfax Avenue, Sassafras serves up delicious dishes inspired by Cajun and Southern cuisines. While Sassafras typically closes around 2:30 p.m., they occasionally extend their hours for special events, making it worth checking their schedule for late-night opportunities. Their menu features dishes like shrimp and grits, chicken and waffles, and beignets. Prices are moderate, and the restaurant's charming décor creates a warm and inviting setting for a night out.

Denver Biscuit Company:

The Denver Biscuit Company, known for its mouthwatering biscuits and Southern-inspired dishes, offers a late-night menu at select locations. Whether you're in the mood for a hearty biscuit sandwich or a plate of fried chicken and biscuits, you'll find plenty of options to satisfy your cravings. With locations in Denver and Colorado Springs, the Denver Biscuit Company is a convenient spot for a late-night bite. Hours vary by location, but some branches are open until midnight or later on weekends. The relaxed, casual atmosphere makes it an ideal hangout spot for groups of friends.

Illegal Pete's:
Illegal Pete's is a regional chain known for its burritos, bowls, and tacos. With locations in Denver, Boulder, Fort Collins, and other parts of Colorado, Illegal Pete's is a popular choice for a late-night meal. Most locations are open until midnight or later, making it a great option for those looking for a hearty meal after a night out. The menu offers a variety of customizable options, from vegetarian and vegan choices to hearty meat-filled dishes. Prices are reasonable, and the lively, laid-back atmosphere makes it a great place to hang out with friends.

Union Lodge No. 1:
For those seeking a late-night cocktail spot, Union Lodge No. 1 in downtown Denver offers an elegant setting and a menu of meticulously crafted cocktails. The bar's vintage-inspired décor and attention to detail create a sophisticated atmosphere, perfect for a nightcap. Union Lodge No. 1 typically closes around 2:00 a.m., making it an excellent option for those looking to enjoy a drink late into the night.

CLOSING THOUGHTS AND INSIDER TIPS

As we've come to the final pages of this ultimate travel guide to Colorado, I hope that the insights, tips, and recommendations shared throughout these pages have inspired you to embark on your own adventure in the Centennial State. From the rugged peaks of the Rocky Mountains to the bustling streets of Denver and the quaint mountain towns in between, Colorado offers a wealth of experiences for travelers of all interests and preferences. One of the most striking aspects of Colorado is its diverse landscape, which ranges from towering mountains to rolling plains and everything in between. Whether you're an outdoor enthusiast seeking adrenaline-pumping thrills or a culture aficionado looking to explore vibrant art scenes and historical landmarks, Colorado has it all. Each region of the state offers its own unique charm and attractions, ensuring that every visit is filled with new experiences and unforgettable memories.

As a veteran traveler and author, I can attest to the transformative power of exploring new destinations firsthand. And in Colorado, there's no shortage of opportunities to immerse yourself in the wonders of nature, embrace thrilling outdoor adventures, and discover the rich cultural heritage that defines this remarkable state. Remember to take the time to venture off the beaten path, explore hidden gems, and connect with the local communities that call Colorado home. Whether you're hiking through pristine wilderness, sampling local cuisine, or attending a lively festival, each experience will enrich your understanding of this diverse and dynamic destination.

As you prepare for your journey, keep in mind the insider tips shared throughout this guide: immerse yourself in nature, embrace adventure, discover the local culture, prepare for high altitude, and always practice Leave No Trace principles to preserve Colorado's natural beauty for future generations. Above all, approach your travels with an open mind and a spirit of curiosity. Whether you're seeking adrenaline-pumping thrills or peaceful moments of solitude, Colorado has something to offer every traveler. So, pack your bags, hit the road, and get ready to create memories that will last a lifetime in the breathtaking landscapes of Colorado. Safe travels, and may your adventures in the Centennial State be filled with joy, wonder, and unforgettable experiences.

Printed in Great Britain
by Amazon